MW01520476

Forgiveness: The Jesus Way

The Proven Path To Be Forgiving And Forgiven

James K. Wagner

CSS Publishing Company, Inc., Lima, Ohio

FORGIVENESS: THE JESUS WAY

Library of Congress Cataloging-in-Publication Data

Wagner, James K.
    Forgiveness : the Jesus way : the proven path to be forgiving and forgiven / James K. Wagner.
      p. cm.
    Includes bibliographical references.
    ISBN 0-7880-2437-X (perfect bound : alk. paper)
    1. Forgiveness—Religious aspects—Christianity. I. Title.

BV4647.F55W34 2007
234'.5—dc22

2006101960

For more information about CSS Publishing Company resources, visit our website at www.csspub.com or email us at custserv@csspub.com or call (800) 241-4056.

ISBN-13: 978-0-7880-2437-5
ISBN-10: 0-7880-2437-X
PRINTED IN U.S.A.

For Laurie, Kerrie, Toby — my children
who taught their father many lessons
in the art and practice of giving
and receiving forgiveness

Forgiveness is taking seriously the awfulness of what has happened when you are treated unfairly. It is opening the door for the person to have a chance to begin again.

— Archbishop Desmond Tutu

Table Of Contents

Prologue

Who Am I?

I am highly sought after, but strangely elusive.

I am taught faithfully to children, but rarely lived by the tutors.

I am romanticized in poem and novel, but seldom seen in everyday life.

I am first cousin to mercy and love, but all too absent in the human family.

I am related to forgetting, but not kin to amnesia.

I am a key to good health, but hardly used to unlock benefits unlimited.

I am an antidote for dealing with stress-filled relationships, but kept hidden in resentful hearts.

I am the topic of many sermons, but living examples are hard to come by.

Though I am not impossible, I am perceived to be improbable and impractical.

Most everyone expresses a need for me, but no one wants to go first.

Some have called me a chance to start over, a sign of hope, a medicine that can cure this world's ills.

WHO AM I?

I am a gift from God for giving to others.

I am a gift from God for receiving from others.

I AM FORGIVENESS!

Foreword

As a young theological student, and then pastor, in the late 1950s, I had never read a book on the power of forgiveness and its relationship to our physical and emotional health. Such books were rare. The few that did explore the practical application of forgiveness were generally considered theologically questionable.

As best I can recall, no class I took in seminary ever discussed forgiveness at depth theologically, psychologically, exegetically, homiletically, or liturgically. And there *were no* classes on contemporary spirituality.

Forgiveness was, of course, mentioned in sermons. I remember writing and preaching a sermon on forgiveness in my senior year at theological school. I spoke of forgiveness as a Christian virtue, a duty, enjoined by scripture; something we all ought to do as an act of will as soon as possible. I am sure I quoted a lot of poetry.

It did not occur to me to explain *why* forgiveness was enjoined by scripture. I did not explain that it was an emotional, spiritual need, a foundational aspect of our human wholeness. Nor did I explain just *how* one can move healthfully through the difficult steps and stages of forgiving. I did not explain it, because I did not know it.

How much it would have helped me as a young minister if such a book as James Wagner's *Forgiveness: The Jesus Way* had come into my hands. How deeply my ministry and my personal life would have been enriched.

One need only glance at Wagner's bibliography to see an almost explosive proliferation of forgiveness literature in recent decades. Books, workshops, retreats, journals, and videos authorized by secular movements, as well as spiritual, offer us research results and new insights on this journey of release we call forgiveness. So what makes James Wagner's book so special? Why does it stand out so significantly amidst this recent abundance? I see five major aspects.

First, the power of the biblical rootedness of this book. Those who have read Wagner's books on healing have long depended on his scriptural foundation and depth. All that he writes is embedded in the biblical witness. He is far from being a rigid biblical literalist, but he makes clear the thrust of God's presence and purpose throughout scripture. A clear luminosity shines from the biblical texts of Jesus' teachings and acts of forgiveness.

Second, the power of the book's sensitivity to the issues of the human heart, its wounds, hurts, and longings. Nowhere in this book do we find the dangerously simplistic concepts of forgiveness which are still so widespread. Wagner examines each of these concepts and reveals how ineffectual and dangerous they are. He understands the pain, anger, and bitterness we carry that makes forgiveness a near impossibility for so many. *He sees the problem.*

Third, the power of the book's realism and awareness of the justice issues that are so often overlooked. There is nothing sentimental about this book. Wagner neither ignores or overrides abuse and injustice. He is keenly aware of atrocities that must be faced and named. He is aware (as so many are not) that abuse and atrocity may make reconciliation and restored relationship unlikely in this world if willingness to be healed remains one-sided. But even in the midst of such brokenness, Wagner reveals ways by which we may release ourselves from the emotional and spiritual prisons of destructive bitterness.

Fourth, the power of the book's practicality. So many books and sermons, even in these days, speak of the necessity, the beauty, the healthfulness of forgiveness, but do not tell us just *how* to forgive. They show us metaphorical pictures of that beautiful country of release, the freedom that will be ours, as well as the peace and improved health we will feel. They point out, frighteningly, the physical, emotional, and spiritual dangers of not being in that realm, but they give us no map of the way. Forgiveness is not an act of willpower, neither is it a sudden mystical breaking of the bonds. Wagner shows us the steps of the divine process by which the impossibility becomes possible.

Fifth, the power of the book's relevance to our contemporary society. Here is no dreamy wish fulfillment. Wagner presents reality, backed by research and fact-finding. I am impressed by his full use of contemporary surveys, both medical and sociological, and the way he draws upon recent research to illustrate the effects of the release of forgiveness upon our bodies and minds.

As the peoples of this world draw perilously close in hurt and hatred as well as helpfulness, as our power to destroy races against our power of compassion, God send that such books as this of empowered healing reach many hands.

— Flora S. Wuellner

Flora Slesson Wuellner, an ordained minister of the United Church of Christ, is well known throughout the United States and Europe for her writings and retreat leadership that focus on inner healing. Wuellner was educated at the University of Michigan and at Chicago Theological Seminary. She is a contributor to *The Upper Room.*

Acknowledgments

Because the human complexities of forgiveness issues do not lend themselves to "pat answers," this has been a highly challenging and at times exhausting book to research and write. Without the prayers, encouragement, and assistance of many people, this book could not have been completed. Therefore, my genuine gratitude and appreciation:

- To Gaylord Reed and David Warner for their technical expertise and help with the vagaries of computers and word processing.

- To Dr. William Thiele, pastoral counselor, for his insights and practical guidelines.

- To Doris Donnelly, Flora Wuellner, and Marjorie Thompson, whose published writings on forgiveness continue to inspire, motivate, and keep me focused.

- To Karen Franz, secretary at Columbia Heights United Methodist Church in Columbus, Ohio, for her generous time and office assistance with the manuscript.

- To those Christian friends, gathered for Disciplined Order of Christ retreats, who were the first to read and discuss the material in this book. Their suggestions, well received by the author, strengthened the manuscript.

- To a host of knowledgeable persons whose recommended forgiveness resources proved to be invaluable.

- To my wife, Mary Lou, whose intuitive comments and loving companionship kept me "at it."

— James K. Wagner

Introduction

If I were to name the most emotionally entangled sickness, a worldwide, crippling unhealthiness, an illness extremely difficult to cure, I would point to a resentful, unforgiving heart and the intentional withholding of forgiveness. As a Christian minister actively engaged in a Christ-centered ministry of healing and wholeness since the 1960s, I have counseled and prayed with hundreds of people who expressed every imaginable kind of illness. Would it surprise you to know that approximately fifty percent of those who request healing prayer ask for help, not for their physical pains and limitations, but rather for their spiritual, emotional, and mental anguish over damaged and fractured relationships?

When we carry deep hurts by others, when we harbor resentment, revenge, jealousy, anger, and hateful attitudes, when we are unwilling to give or to receive forgiveness, we are positioning ourselves for agonizing problems and a host of potential personal illnesses.

Whereas forgiveness is a key that opens the door to avenues of good health and a more satisfying life, unforgiveness keeps the door locked on a self-imposed, critical, unbending, legalistic, I-know-I'm-right outlook on life. Some think they are doing another a favor by offering forgiveness. Truth is, forgiveness blesses the giver more than it benefits the receiver. This is sometimes called "the boomerang effect." The forgiving attitude and action bring positive returns. However, "the boomerang effect" is also operative when forgiveness is withheld causing a negative impact on the unforgiver.

Those who are acquainted with the teaching of Jesus know that he expects his disciples to model a forgiveness lifestyle. Yet, Christians soon discover that forgiveness is as demanding and as difficult for them as it is for non-Christians. Why? What are some of the reasons forgiveness seems next to impossible at times? Why can't Christians simply forgive and forget easily and without hesitation? What causes the gap between our knowledge of the biblical guidelines and our personal unwillingness to be forgiving people?

This book not only explores these and related issues, but also invites you, the reader, to examine your own understandings and practices of forgiveness. Together let us take an unhurried look at the various ways Jesus modeled forgiveness by personal example and by his teachings. Together let us learn to be more merciful, forgiving human beings. Together let us grow to appreciate and practice forgiveness:

- a gift of God's grace and mercy.
- a gift to give others and to receive from others.
- a gift that is good medicine for all humanity.
- a gift that makes possible that seemingly impossible petition in the Lord's Prayer, "and forgive us our debts, as we also have forgiven our debtors."

Suggestions For Personal Study

The first four sessions present facts and facets of forgiveness. The last eight sessions focus on the forgiveness paradigm of Jesus. Each session presents several options and patterns, but keep in mind that there is no perfect method to engage in the forgiveness process.

Read and study all parts of this book with a notepad at hand to record your personal responses, reactions, questions, and comments. If you are not in a group study, it is highly recommended that you contact someone whom you trust who would be available to meet with you, as the need arises, to discuss your personal forgiveness issues. Approach this book with a genuine desire to learn and a personal readiness to live the Jesus way of forgiveness.

Group Study Guide

Twelve sessions are outlined for group study and discussions. The group guides are found at the end of each session. To get your heart and mind around the Jesus way of forgiveness, the author recommends that you read completely through the book without rushing or skipping pages and, with a notebook close by, record your thoughts and insights. Then return to the study guides for a second reading and renewed openness to the Jesus way of forgiveness. One person may lead or coordinate the entire study, or group members may take turns leading from session to session. Group leaders need to be flexible and sensitive to the personal situation of each group member, especially in times of sharing and praying. Because forgiveness/unforgiveness can be highly complex and not always subject to quick-fixes, remind each one in the group to come together with compassion, sensitivity, and mutual respect. Confidentiality within the group must be honored and guarded by all. To foster participation, ownership, and accountability, invite the group members to covenant (agree)

- to be present for all sessions;
- to meet once a week, if at all possible;
- to pray for one another daily;
- to read, study, and reflect on the assigned material in preparation for each meeting;
- to express disagreements and various opinions in an atmosphere of mutual support;
- to come to each meeting with a loving heart, an open mind, and a teachable spirit;
- to saturate each session with prayer, allowing the focus of prayers to arise from the felt needs and life situations of the moment; and
- to set time limits for each meeting (no less than one hour or more than two).[1]

A word for the session leaders: Review the study guide for each session before the group meetings. Develop a lesson plan. Be sensitive to your time limits. Be flexible. If your group would like to continue meeting after completing this book, you are invited to review and consider the Recommended Resources at the back of the book.

True/False Quiz

Forgiveness is the answer to the child's dream of a
miracle by which what is broken is made whole again,
what is soiled is made clean again.

— Dag Hammarskjold

Take a few minutes to respond to these twelve true or false statements. This test is not intended to give simple answers to difficult questions, but rather to provide a snapshot of the complicated landscape inhabited by forgiveness and non-forgiveness issues.

1. Forgiveness is contrary to human nature.
2. Only with God's help is forgiveness possible.
3. Forgiveness is one of Jesus' most mentioned topics.
4. Jesus only taught one way to forgive.
5. Forgiveness means to forgive and forget.
6. Forgiveness is a process not to be rushed.
7. Forgiveness is an act of the heart (the emotions) not a decision of the mind (the intellect).
8. Accepting an apology can be more difficult than offering an apology.
9. Forgiving one's self is fairly easy to do.
10. Some people have a need to forgive God.
11. Forgiving someone who has died is not possible.
12. To give to another person before that person gives to you is to forgive.

Compare your answers to those on the following pages.

Answers To The True/False Quiz
1. Forgiveness is contrary to human nature. True

The foundational fact is that basic human nature is not characterized by "turning the other cheek," "praying for one's enemies," or "loving those who persecute you" (Matthew 5:39, 44). We come into this world with an inborn, tigerish desire to protect ourselves and guard our possessions at all costs. Observe pre-school children at play. One child, for whatever reason, strikes another child, who in turn strikes back ("an eye for an eye, a tooth for a tooth" Matthew 5:38). These children grow up, are introduced to Jesus, and are taught Jesus' teachings about the importance of forgiving one another. They make personal commitments to be lifelong Christians. Does that then make it easier for these maturing adults to give and receive forgiveness? No and yes! No, it's not going to be an automatic forgiveness response in every situation because the Christian still must deal with his or her basic human nature. Yes, it can be easier if the Christian who is hurt by another makes a conscious decision to not live in the past, to offer forgiveness, to attempt reconciliation, and move on in life. Knowing how and why to forgive must be coupled with a sincere desire to forgive.

2. Only with God's help is forgiveness possible. True

Here is another facet sparkling on the face of forgiveness. Consequently any desire to engage in an act of forgiveness needs to be bathed in prayer for God's help, wisdom, and guidance. Not to call on God would indeed be non-productive. Human resources alone rarely mend a broken heart or relationship. Consider the often quoted English poet/philosopher Alexander Pope: "To err is human, to forgive divine."[2] Some have interpreted this wise saying to mean, since only God can forgive, why should human beings even attempt it? This can become a rationale to disengage in any kind reconciling actions, especially in the worst case scenarios of inhuman behavior and violence. "Maybe God can do it, but there is no way I'm going to forgive _____." Sound familiar?

While traveling late one afternoon, my wife and I stopped at a roadside cafe for coffee. Coming out of the restaurant as we were entering was a big, burly, rough looking character wearing a soiled, white T-shirt with these eye-catching words: "To err is human. To forgive is out of the question."

On the human level alone, yes, forgiveness is out of the question. However, "if forgiveness is divine, then it is not an act of [human] willpower but an operation of [God's] grace."[3]

To forgive is not out of the question because of the life, mission, and ministry of Jesus Christ who provides access to God's grace and ever-present help in all circumstances.

3. Forgiveness is one of Jesus' most mentioned topics. True

Jesus' primary mission was to proclaim by teaching, preaching, and healing that the kingdom of God was at hand. The Master Teacher illustrated this basic message with dozens of stories (parables) and with his personal lifestyle. Keep in mind that the kingdom of God is a realm, a state of existence that calls for everyone to live in right relationships with God and with people. When asked to respond to the question: "Teacher, which commandment in the law is the greatest?" Jesus said, "You shall love the Lord your God with all your heart, and with all your soul, and with all your mind. This is the greatest and first commandment. And a second is like it: 'You shall love your neighbor as yourself' " (Matthew 22:36-39). No doubt Jesus knew that life's many relationships would be violated, abused, and mistreated. This is why a significant amount of his teachings deal with forgiveness as an effective therapy. This book invites you to take an unhurried, in-depth look at eight of Jesus' forgiveness teachings in Sessions 5-12.

4. Jesus only taught one way to forgive. False

Some might answer TRUE to this statement based on the mandate by Jesus to his disciples during their final meal together:

> *I give you a new commandment, that you love one another. Just as I have loved you, you also should love one another. By this everyone will know that you are my disciple, if you have love for one another.*
> — John 13:34-35

Granted, Jesus' only commandment ("Love one another") encompasses all of life; however, there are many ways to express our love for one another. Forgiveness is a most effective way to do this and Jesus was quite helpful in outlining several forgiveness patterns. These are recorded in the gospel of Matthew 5:1—7:29, "The Sermon on the Mount," and in the gospel of Luke 6:17-49, "The Sermon on the Plain."

- Pray for those who persecute you.
- Love your enemies.
- Do good to those who hate you.
- Bless those who curse you.
- If anyone strikes you on the cheek, offer the other also.
- Do to others as you would have them do to you.
- Be merciful, just as your Father is merciful.
- Forgive and you will be forgiven.
- Why do you see the speck in your neighbor's eye, but do not notice the log in your own eye?
- When you are offering your gift at the altar, if you remember that your brother or sister has something against you, leave your gift there before the altar and go; first be reconciled, and then come and offer your gift.

Jesus taught and demonstrated many methods and strategies of forgiveness.

5. Forgiveness means to forgive and forget. True and False

This is a tricky one. Conventional wisdom says that if you cannot do both, forgive and forget, then you really have not forgiven. However, amnesia is not the Christian's goal. We do not ask God to erase the memory tapes of our past life. It is totally unrealistic to expect God to blank-out certain episodes in our personal history. The forgiveness process is complete when we can recall the hurtful person or damaging event without remembering or feeling the pain, the injury, and the distress associated with that person or event. One benefit of our God-given memories is not to repeat harmful actions or to associate with persons who hurt us. Archbishop Desmond Tutu has a helpful insight:

Forgiveness does not mean amnesia. Amnesia is a most dangerous thing, especially on a community, national, or international level. We must forgive, but almost always we should not forget that there were atrocities, because if we do, we are then likely to repeat those atrocities. Those who forgive and those who accept forgiveness must not forget in their reconciling. If we don't deal with our past adequately, it will return to haunt us.[4]

Therefore, question 5 has a double answer:
1. True ... Forgiveness means to forgive and forget the painful memories.
2. False ... Forgiveness means to forgive, but not forget the event, the circumstance, or the people surrounding past episodes in our life. To forget the pain, but not the past is a realistic possibility.

6. Forgiveness is a process not to be rushed. True

Another way to phrase this: Forgiveness takes time. How much time? That depends on the situation. Keep in mind that time is not the healing agent. The value of time is that it gives some space and distance to the one who has been hurt. Time is often needed to sort out the real problem, to understand what needs to be forgiven, and to decide some possible next steps in the forgiveness process.

When the United States entered World War II, following the Japanese attack on Pearl Harbor on December 7, 1941, forgiveness was out of the question. Likewise, when the war ended in August 1945 with the US dropping of the atomic bombs. Now, well over a half-century later Japan and the United states are at peace, with citizens welcome to travel in each other's country, and profitable trading markets benefiting each nation. Although untold numbers of American and Japanese families have yet to heal the emotional scars and wounds of war, the relationship between the two countries has improved immensely. It takes time to forgive fully and to let go of the hurt completely. How do you know when forgiveness is complete and the time is up? When you can remember the harmful episode or the person or family who hurt you without getting an upset stomach or severe headache or an overload of resentment and bitterness. Forgiveness is an ongoing process not a momentary event. To forgive too quickly is to forgive prematurely.

7. Forgiveness is an act of the heart (the emotions) not a decision of the mind (the intellect). False
This facet of forgiveness suffers from widespread misunderstanding. Some would label question 7 as true. Some would say, "Forgiveness is an act of the heart because forgiveness is an emotional experience, a feeling of being sorry." If you always wait until you feel like forgiving someone, chances are you will wait a long, long time and may never get around to forgiving that person. Emotions and feelings do not change quickly; whereas, our mind reacts and responds much faster. True, forgiveness can be an emotional experience, but the first step in the forgiveness process begins with a conscious act, a decision of the mind. It may take our emotions, our feelings, our stomach several days or weeks to catch up and accept what the mind decides to do.

> *I choose to forgive* _____. *I will forgive*
> _____. *Even though I may not feel like forgiving, I know that as a Christian, Jesus wants me to forgive whether I feel like it or not.*

Keep in mind that the personal determination to get started on the forgiveness process is directly linked to the time-factor in Number 6. There is usually a time span between the moment of being hurt and the decision to forgive and move on. When we are hurt very deeply, painfully violated, or abused repeatedly, the desire to forgive can be totally absent. Such unthinkable, inhuman situations happen all too frequently. So what is a Christian to do?

Consider praying a pre-forgiveness prayer each day, something like this:

> *O God, I can't do it. I simply can't forgive _____.*
> *I'm not even sure what to do next. Help me get through this. And help me to be willing to forgive someday, not today, and probably not tomorrow, but some day. Amen.*

24

A pre-forgiveness prayer is realistic and helpful because it acknowledges the personal damage, is fully aware of the problem, turns to God for divine guidance in getting through this mess, and asks God to hasten the day when a forgiving attitude might be possible.

8. Accepting an apology can be more difficult than offering an apology. True

An apology is a gift of special words or actions that express a sincere, repentant attitude.

> *Will you accept my apology for the trouble I have caused? I apologize for hurting you. Will you forgive me?*

To accept an apology is to accept a unique gift that presents hopeful possibilities in the forgiveness process. To reject an apology is to shut the door on new beginnings in a relationship. Think of an apology as an unearned, unmerited gift. To receive an apology may be more difficult than to offer an apology because the giver has taken the initiative to improve the situation. If the receiver is not ready to do that, then the gift is refused, either temporarily or permanently. How do you respond when someone telephones and says: "I just called to tell you I'm sorry. I'm really sorry. Will you accept my apology?" If you answer, "Oh, just forget it. It was nothing." That could well be interpreted by the caller as a rejection of the apology. It really was "something" to the caller but the receiver's insensitivity was not helpful.

Now consider a more affirming response to the same phone call.

> *Why ... why thank you for calling. I guess you and I have had some misunderstandings or differences. Yes, I accept your apology and I do thank you for calling.*

How well do you accept and receive gifts from others? "The making of an apology," writes L. William Countryman, "is a way of participating in God's gracious and generous project of redeeming the world through the spread of forgiveness. Our apology puts us 'in the way' of forgiveness. It is one contribution we can make when we have wronged another. I do not mean that our repentance earns forgiveness, either from God or from the injured party ... true forgiveness is possible only as a gift, never as payment."[5]

9. Forgiving one's self is fairly easy to do. False

Forgiving one's self is not impossible, but it is difficult. Why? It means we have to admit to ourselves that we are not perfect, we are wrong at times, we are out-of-line, or to use biblical language, we have to face up to our personal sins. That's tough to do! The challenge of forgiving one's self is compounded by the lack of guidelines on how to go about it. How often have we heard a sympathetic friend or counselor say: "Now, what you need to do is forgive yourself." But how? "Just admit your mistakes. Put it all behind you. Forgive yourself and move on." But how? The initial steps in a self-forgiveness process must begin with God and with God's forgiveness of us.

The renowned Quaker author, Douglas Steere, speaks helpfully to those who are serious about self-forgiveness:

> *There is ... a condition for receiving God's gift of forgiveness. [We] must be willing to accept it. Absurd as this may seem, there are few who will believe in and accept the forgiveness of God so completely as to ... leave their sin with God forever. They are always reopening the vault where they have deposited their sin ... forever asking to have it back in order to fondle it; reconstruct, query, or worry over it ... Thus their sin ties them to the past.*[6]

The freedom and release of forgiveness are too often lost to those who are caught in the quagmire of self-condemnation. Underscore, accept, and celebrate this therapeutic, spiritual truth in Romans 8:1-2, "There is therefore now no condemnation for those who are in Christ Jesus. For the law of the Spirit of life in Christ Jesus has set you free from the law of sin and death." For guidelines in the self-forgiveness process, see "Self-Forgiveness" in Session 9.

10. Some people need to forgive God. True

Another way to say this: Some people are so upset with God that they waste many hours being mad at God. For whatever reason, there are those who truly believe that God has been unfair, unkind, and uncaring to them. This negative attitude may persist for years. One day when making a pastoral visit in the home of an elderly widow, I was greeted at the door by her son, Paul, who invited me in, then promptly removed himself from the room.

On subsequent visits, the same scenario took place. I knew that Paul was an inactive member of the church, but had never had a conversation with him. I said to his mother, "Tell me, why is it that when I come Paul does not join us here in the living room?" "Oh, pastor," she said a bit embarrassed, "don't mind Paul. He's mad at God and refuses to come to church. I wish you would have a talk with him."

Several months later, the opportunity presented itself. Paul came to the door, but this time he sat down with me and his mother. In a non-judgmental way, I inquired about his work before he had retired, discovered some of his interesting hobbies, and learned about his favorite television programs. Before I left that afternoon, I offered a word of prayer and blessing. As Paul escorted me to the door, he said, "Thanks for coming. Maybe you and I could get together and talk some time."

Soon after that, Paul came by my office and quickly let me know why he and God were not on speaking terms. "Would you like to do something about that?" I asked. "Like what?" "Well, first of all I want to say that it is okay to be upset with God. On the one hand, I do not believe that God ever wants to harm or hurt us; on the other hand, sometimes our human perception is that God has been unfair or that God plays favorites or that God has been the cause of some personal problems. Your first step would be to be honest with God and tell God how you feel about the way you think God has been treating you. Some of the people in the Bible did that and God did not strike them dead. Check out the prophet

27

Jeremiah who complained bitterly to God (Jeremiah 12:1-4). Some of the psalms (44 and 88) express anger and hostility toward God. Then your next steps might be to forgive God and express a desire to have a better relationship with God." Paul agreed to try this. Now, let's be clear at this point. God did not need to be forgiven, but Paul had a need to forgive God in order to break the impasse and to improve his relationship with God. A few weeks later I began to see Paul in church on Sunday mornings. As Robert Schuller puts it: "Life's not fair, but God is good!"[7]

11. Forgiving someone who has died is not possible. False

Someone whom we love and care about may have died before we got around to offering that apology or making our peace. It's not too late. In a genuine, heart-felt prayer we can call on Jesus Christ to take our message of forgiveness and to communicate our apology and love to those who no longer live on earth. As Christians we declare our belief in the communion of saints, that fellowship of Christ's followers, living and dead. The book of Hebrews gives us hope and encouragement by assuring us that Jesus Christ is our Great High Priest who mediates and communicates on our behalf.

> *Let us therefore approach the throne of grace with boldness, so that we may receive mercy and find grace to help in time of need.* — Hebrews 4:16

This is not a suggestion that we communicate with the dead; rather, this can be helpful therapy for those who have unfinished business connected with their grief in the death of loved ones. The focus is on the risen, universal, compassionate Christ who is quite able to accomplish in the spiritual realm what we are unable to do in the physical arena of life.

12. To give to another person before that person gives to you is to forgive. True

This is a play on words. Note carefully the spelling of *forgive*, *forgiven*, and *forgiveness*. Our inability or stubbornness to take the initiative when forgiveness is called for might lead us to change the spellings to *aftergive*, *aftergiven*, and *aftergiveness*.

- After you make amends and apologize, I will forgive you.
- After you show me that you are sincere, I will forgive.

Go back to the original spelling.

- Before you make amends and apologize, I will forgive.
- Before you show me that you are sincere, I will forgive.

To paraphrase 1 John 4:9-12, "God loved us and gave us Jesus before we knew what love was about, not *after* we knew." Jesus was a giving and a forgiving person who expects his followers to be giving and forgiving human beings. To give to another person *before* that person gives to us is to *forgive*. That's the Jesus way!

A Prayer For Becoming Recipients
And Channels Of Forgiveness

Heavenly Father, we confess that we are quicker to ask you to forgive us than we are to forgive others. We allow hidden animosity to deposit a steady stream of poison into the bloodstream of our thoughts; we repeatedly reenact past hurts in our minds until they are vivid and painful, over and over again.

We rekindle the embers of the unhappy past until they burst forth into new flames of bitterness. We nurse our grievances, feeding and pampering them until they grow into monsters which destroy the good. We overload our minds with slights and oversights, insults and judgments, until we carry around a constant burden of resentments. As a result of all this, Lord, our outlook becomes dim, our minds become clouded, our bodies become tired, and our spirits become shriveled.

Teach us anew, Father, that the manner in which we forgive others is inseparable from the manner in which you forgive us. May we soon become not only recipients of your forgiving love, but channels by which that forgiveness is conveyed to others. In Jesus' name. Amen.[8]

Session I

The True/False Quiz

Study Guide

1. Opening prayer by the group leader.

2. Take a few moments to introduce each member of the group.

3. Review your personal responses to the twelve statements.

4. Invite group discussion around the author's answers.

5. What are some issues and questions related to forgiveness that you do not find in this quiz? Discuss.

6. Closure
   - Read aloud the Group Study Guide on pages 16-17.
   - Decide on the leadership for each session.
   - Set the days and times for the group meetings.
   - Invite the group members to volunteer to lead opening prayer in each session.
   - Pray together: "A Prayer For Becoming Recipients And Channels Of Forgiveness" (p. 29).

7. Homework: Pray for one another and study "What Is Forgiveness?" (Session 2)

Session 2

What Is Forgiveness?

Forgiveness: To stop feeling angry or resentful towards someone for an offence, flaw, or mistake.
— *The New Oxford English Dictionary*, 1998

Forgive, forgiven, and *forgiveness* are words commonly used but seldom defined. Frequently we are told that we need to be more forgiving, but hardly ever shown how to go about it, or why it is beneficial. It is something like this conversation between a Sunday school teacher and the class of third grade girls and boys.

Teacher: "Who can tell me what love is?"

Young boy: "I'm not sure exactly, but I know it when I see it."

Not quite satisfied with that answer, the teacher tried it again. "Who can tell me what love is?"

This time a young girl raised her hand: "Teacher, I'm not real sure either, but I do know my Mom and Dad are in it."

The same thing could well be said about the popular understanding or misunderstanding of forgiveness. We are not quite sure what it is, but we recognize it when we see it or experience it.

Let's begin with the biblical definitions of *forgive, forgiven,* and *forgiveness*. These words are used over 100 times in the Bible, a clear witness to their significance (51 in the Hebrew scriptures of the Old Testament and 58 in the Greek scriptures of the New Testament). Notice that the root of these words, in both the Hebrew and the Greek, has similar translations in English:

> *to lay aside, to pardon, to give up, to yield, to let alone, to release, to spare, to grant a favor, to give freely, to rescue, to deliver, to set free, to cancel debt, to forgive.*[9]

So what is forgiveness? Granted that any one definition or description of forgiveness would be inadequate, consider several excellent insights.

> *To forgive is to make a conscious choice to release the person who has wounded us from the sentence of our judgment, however justified that judgment may be. It represents a choice to leave behind our resentment and desire for retribution, however fair such punishment might seem.*[10]

> *Forgiveness is taking responsibility from my side to release the offender from the alienating effect of the offense on our relationship.*[11]

> *Forgiveness is a major release: a release from the prison and burden of the past. This release does not mean release from responsibility for what was done. Nor does release necessarily mean release from the chains of resentment and guilt that hold us back from entering God's freedom, the new beginning as a beloved child of God. It means release from the expectations and obligations of the past so that we and those who injured us may start anew.*[12]

> *Forgiveness is a mystery. It belongs to the realm of freedom rather than the realm of necessity; it is scented with the spices of grace rather than the sweat of legalism; it delights and humbles with the impact of wholly unexpected bounty; gentler than a tender embrace, it is tougher than the bands of retribution that strap us tightly to our pain.*[13]

> *Forgiveness is God's invention for coming to terms with a world in which, despite their best intentions, people are unfair to each other and hurt each other deeply ... Forgiving is love's toughest work, and love's biggest risk. If you twist it into something it was never meant to*

be, it can make you a doormat or an insufferable ma-
nipulator. Forgiving seems almost unnatural. Our sense
of fairness tells us people should pay for the wrong they
do. But forgiving is love's power to break nature's rule.[14]

These thoughtful descriptions paint a positive picture of forgiveness. However, we also need to consider this partial list of popular misconceptions.

Forgiveness is not ...

• covering up the conflict,
• peaceful co-existence,
• making excuses for bad behavior,
• tolerating the situation,
• condoning unkindness and harmful actions,
• trying to forget,
• self-sacrifice,
• denying our hurts and feelings,
• being a long-suffering martyr,
• setting conditional limits, or
• smiling no matter what happens.

If you have practiced any of the above, even with good inten-
tions and in the name of forgiveness, then you have discovered
their frustrating and discouraging limitations. This thought by Henri
J. M. Nouwen offers yet another facet of forgiveness and preparation for entering the complex drama of reconciliation scenarios.

Forgiveness is the name of love practiced among people
who love poorly. The hard truth is that all of us love
poorly. We do not even know what we are doing when
we hurt others. We need to forgive and be forgiven ev-
ery day, every hour — unceasingly. That is the great
work of love among the fellowship of the weak that is
the human family.[15]

Steps In Forgiveness

Forgiver A — Dr. Doris Donnelly, author, educator, and retreat leader. In addition to teaching in several colleges and universities in the United States, Dr. Donnelly has served as a consultant in the area of adult education for various Roman Catholic Dioceses. The outline that follows is taken from lecture notes while participating in her workshops.

The Three-Step Process Of Forgiveness

1. I am hurt or I have hurt someone. My feelings get hurt. Someone whom I care about really upsets me.
2. I name the hurtful issue and choose to forgive. I decide what strategy I will use to forgive the other person.
3. I attempt reconciliation. I try to bring together separated relationships.

Our basic human tendency is not to go beyond Step One. The more natural reaction is to ignore the problem, or to pout, sulk, get mad, and begin plotting ways to get even, or to offer a superficial apology, trying to smooth things over quickly and not deal with the deeper issues. However, thoughtful consideration needs to be given to alternate choices.

The Jesus way of forgiveness chooses to forgive and moves on to Step Two. Be sensitive to the "time-element" between Step One and Step Two. It may take five minutes, five days, five years, or longer. Time does not heal, but time offers needed space to deal with one's damaged feelings and to identify what is really going on in the fractured relationship. In other words, to move too quickly from Step One to Step Two is not helpful. To never move from Step One to Step Two is worse. The most crucial part of Step Two is deciding how to go about forgiving the one who hurt you. Jesus taught us several forgiveness strategies, such as: praying for one's enemy, turning the other cheek, doing good to those who persecute you, and confronting the other person with the hurtful issues. Other options could be writing a letter, sending an email message, making a sincere apology, a phone call, or a personal visit. The strategies of communicating for-giveness are many. It is always wise to seek the guidance of the Holy Spirit when being proactive in the forgiveness process.

Step Three is a worthy goal, but not achievable if the other person does not want to be reconciled. We definitely attempt and pray for reconciliation. We thank God for those special times of healing broken relationships. Being realistic, however, you need to remember that the only person you have any control over is your-self. You may have to move on with your life without having been reconciled.

For further exploration of Dr. Donnelly's teachings on forgive-ness, I urge you to read her two excellent books: *Learning To For-give* and *Putting Forgiveness Into Practice*.

A sampling from Dr. Donnelly's writings:

> *Forgiveness makes the difference between war and peace, hatred and love, hope and despair. Without for-giveness, hurts grow unchecked and we recycle fail-ures, resentments, bitterness, and mistrust in our lives. With forgiveness, hurts are acknowledged and healed, and we are able to break a mindless cycle of retaliation by saying that the decisions of human life, even when they turn out badly, are not beyond repair. Martin Luther King, Jr. put it this way, "Forgiveness is a catalyst cre-ating the atmosphere necessary for a fresh start and a new beginning."*[16]

> *Non-forgiveness is a way of reaffirming death; forgive-ness is a way of reaffirming life.*[17]

Forgiver B — Harry Camp, a practicing attorney at law in Tennes-see, dedicated to Jesus Christ and his teachings. An active member of the United Methodist church, he has held various leadership roles in several church renewal ministries. In recent years, he has developed a systematic way to engage in forgiveness. This proce-dure requires time, effort, energy, desire, and miracles of grace.

A Seven-Step Process Of Forgiveness

1. Pray for the desire to forgive.
2. With pencil and paper make a list of all grievances against a particular person, organization, or institution — itemize — be specific. It may take several days for everything to surface in your memory. Ask God to bring these things to mind.
3. Ask God to enable and empower you to forgive. Then go down the list, item by item, and say aloud, "By the grace of God, I forgive you of that."
4. The next day go down the list again. If you have peace about an item, go to the next one. Do this every day until you can look squarely at each item and know that it causes no negative emotions.
5. Put the paper away for a week. Then go down the list one more time and make sure you are not hanging on to any grievance.
6. When you are sure that you have no negative feelings, take scissors and cut the list into pieces, put them in a paper sack, twist the top and put it away for a month. Then hold the sack, remembering its contents. If you experience joy and no bad feelings, burn the sack and its contents.
7. Then thank God for removing your anger and resentment and for giving you the grace of forgiveness, peace, and joy.

(**Note:** You may need to repeat some of the steps before completing the process. This symbolic exercise, when practiced with sincerity and honesty, is very helpful and effective.)[18]

Closing Prayer

We thank you, God of grace and mercy, for your patience with our stubbornness, for your loving consistency with our inconsistencies, for giving so generously to each of us when we are not deserving, for calling us together and helping us not only to come into new understandings of forgiveness, but also empowering us to move out of our self-imposed prisons of resentment, anger, and bitterness and into the liberating freedom of your compassion. In the name of Jesus Christ, who taught us the way to forgive and whose life revealed how to forgive. Amen.

What Is Forgiveness?

Study Guide

1. Begin with a minute of silence, followed with opening prayer.

2. Ask each person to write down a one-sentence definition or description of "forgiveness" and "unforgiveness." Do not rush.

3. Invite those who are willing to share with the group their two definitions.

4. Read "What Is Forgiveness?" in this session. Read aloud the literal translations of "forgiveness" in the Bible. Invite responses and comments.

5. We tend to think of forgiveness as an event, a decision of the moment, something to do as quickly as possible; whereas authors on this challenging topic are united in declaring forgiveness to be a process, or a series of recommended steps.

    Have the group review "The Three-Step Process Of Forgiveness" by Doris Donnelly.

    - I am hurt or I have hurt someone.
    - I name the hurtful issue and choose to forgive.
    - I attempt reconciliation.

    Clarify each step in the forgiveness process. Then invite the group to work silently for a few moments by recalling forgiveness issues they have had in the past and applying Donnelly's Three-Step Process. Discuss.

6. Closing prayer (p. 36).

7. Homework

Pray for one another and study "Health Benefits" in Session 3.

Read the "Seven-Step Process Of Forgiveness" by Harry Camp and do this exercise privately.

Session 3

Health Benefits

A well-known psychoanalyst in England caused widespread comment by the advice she gave numerous patients. "Go (to church) and hear (about) forgiveness of sins." And why not? There must be forgiveness if there is to be health. — G. Ernest Thomas

Not only is forgiveness beneficial in harmonizing our relationships with God and with other people; it is also good medicine for our physical, mental, and emotional well-being. The reverse side of that bold claim is equally true: intentional unforgiveness promotes personal unhealthiness. Why is that? Highly charged emotions and negative personal feelings are released when trusted relationships are violated, broken, or abused. Take a few moments to reflect on these two lists. Identify in both columns those emotions and feelings you have experienced.

Unforgiveness can release	Forgiveness can bring
Anger	Calm
Shame	Joy
Bitterness	Mercy
Guilt	Relief
Embarrassment	Delight
Revenge	Compassion
Depression	Peacefulness
Ingratitude	Thankfulness
Jealousy	Acceptance
Hate	Grace
Close-mindedness	Open-mindedness
Negative attitudes	Positive attitudes

Cursing	Blessing
Intolerance	Love
Hopelessness	Faith
Suspicion	Trust
Resentment	Appreciation
Bondage	Freedom

Forgiveness research is a budding science, attracting increasing numbers of investigators who are motivated to explore the relationship between forgiveness and health. Initial scientific studies are affirming the healing power of forgiveness. Dr. Fred Luskin, a pioneer in forgiveness research and cofounder/director of the Stanford University Forgiveness Project, is convinced that "learning to forgive is good for both your mental and physical well-being and your relationships."[19]

He cites a study at the University of Wisconsin, Madison, that showed the amount of forgiveness people felt was related to their reporting a variety of disease conditions. The more forgiving people were, the less they suffered from a wide range of illnesses. The less forgiving people reported a greater number of health problems. This relationship held constant for both short-term physical complaints and longer-term general well-being ... People who had a higher capacity for forgiveness reported fewer symptoms than those with a less developed ability to forgive. People with higher capacities for forgiveness also reported fewer medically diagnosed chronic conditions. This study established a fundamental relationship between learning to forgive and reported incidences of health complaints.[20]

Another study that focused on forgiveness and health was completed at the University of Tennessee. One hundred seven college students, who had been deeply hurt either by a parent, friend, or romantic partner, were asked to recall the event, and then their blood pressure, heart rate, forehead muscle tension, and sweatiness were measured. The study found that the people who forgave the betrayal had decreased blood pressure, muscle tension, and heart rates when compared to those who had not. The forgivers also reported less stress in their lives and fewer physical symptoms of illness.[21]

Carefully consider these scientific findings:

- People who are more forgiving report fewer health problems.
- Forgiveness leads to less stress and fewer physical symptoms of stress.
- Failure to forgive may be more important than hostility as a risk factor for heart disease.
- People who blame other people for their troubles have higher incidences of illnesses such as cardiovascular disease and cancers.
- People who imagine not forgiving someone show negative changes in blood pressure, muscle tension, and immune response.
- People who imagine forgiving their offender note immediate improvement in their cardiovascular, muscular, and nervous systems.
- Even people with devastating losses can learn to forgive and feel better psychologically and emotionally.[22]

Another connection between forgiveness and one's personal state of health is the damaging effects of sin and guilt. The author of Psalm 32 speaks for generations of people past and present:

> *While I kept silence (about my sin), my body wasted away through my groaning all day long. For day and night your hand was heavy upon me; my strength was dried up as by the heat of summer.* — Psalm 32:3-4

Do you recognize the psalmist's description of guilt's influence on mind and body? Here is a picture of "a nervous wreck." Fill in the details. The psalmist cannot eat, cannot relax, and cannot sleep. Insomnia and lack of appetite are causing weight loss, drained energy, and emotional depression. Although the exact sin is not named, experience teaches that sin by any name can exert a harmful influence on the sinner. The picture brightens:

Then I acknowledged my sin to you [O Lord], and I did not hide my iniquity; I said, "I will confess my transgressions to the Lord. And you [O Lord] forgave the guilt of my sin." — Psalm 32:5

Release and help came only after the psalmist was willing to admit the need for forgiveness. Knowing that this is the way God's mercy and grace work, what prevents us from admitting our guilt, confessing our sin, and allowing God to forgive us? The answer comes in Psalm 32:9.

Do not be like a horse or a mule, without understanding, whose temper must be curbed with bit and bridle.... — Psalm 32:9

Call it stubbornness, bullheadedness, or pride, trying to live with sin and guilt is totally unhealthy.[23]

In his scientifically researched book, *The Faith Factor: Proof Of The Healing Power Of Prayer*, Dr. Dale A. Matthews seeks to revive the twin traditions of healing: science and religion. This practicing physician is convinced that

Carrying the burden of guilty feelings can literally make us sick. As a physician, I have often witnessed patients' transformations once they have "confessed" a dark, long-held secret to me or to a trusted spiritual adviser. In both Judaism and Christianity, believers are urged to confess their sins and repent, and are given formal, regular opportunities to confess and to receive absolution, or assurance of forgiveness. The rhythm of regular confession and absolution, both in group and individual worship, allows us to recognize our mistakes, to share our painful feelings with God and with others, and to turn over a new leaf ... Confession and forgiveness within our religious traditions allow us to learn and to move on, rather than becoming unhealthfully preoccupied with our shortcomings.[24]

A Christian psychiatrist, speaking to a large group of pastors and priests, said, "I wish people would stop confessing their sins in my office. I cannot forgive sin; only God can deal effectively with sin and guilt. I plead with all Christian ministers to offer the forgiveness and love of God in your churches so that people can be truly released from their sin and guilt."[25]

Yes, God is more ready to forgive than we are to confess. Forgiveness of sin and guilt is crucial in the healing process. The health benefits that accompany forgiving attitudes and actions speak for themselves. Developing a forgiving lifestyle is a readily available key to good health.

Three Principles Of Forgiveness

Author's Note: On November 14, 1984, Dr. Anderson Spickard was the guest speaker in The Upper Room Chapel Worship Service, Nashville, Tennessee. At that time, Dr. Spickard was Professor of Medicine at the Vanderbilt Medical Center in the Vanderbilt Institute for Treatment of Addictions. Even though his main focus is working with those who have substance abuse problems, his three principles of forgiveness can also be applied in other situations. Following are my notes taken from his message titled: "Forgiveness As A Form Of Healing."

Three Principles Of Forgiveness In The Recovery And Healing Process

1. Forgive Others — The starting point is to give up, to let go of grudges and resentments. Constantly blaming others for personal problems is a dead-end street.
2. Forgive God — This may not be necessary in every person's circumstances; however, many people blame God for their troubles.
3. Forgive Self — Admit to having made poor choices, accept the consequences of your actions, live in the present and into the future, not in the past.

Dr. Spickard is convinced that within those who have alcohol and drug habits, forgiveness is a universal need and guilt is a universal fact. Being an active Presbyterian, he also believes with conviction that Jesus Christ makes it possible to experience all three forgiveness principles. His scriptural foundations include:

> *It is no longer I who live, but it is Christ who lives in me. And the life I now live in the flesh, I live by faith in the Son of God, who loved me and gave himself for me.*
> — Galatians 2:20

> *My grace is sufficient for you, for my power is made perfect in weakness.* — 2 Corinthians 12:9

> *I can do all things through him (Christ) who strengthens me.* — Philippians 4:13

Dr. Anderson Spickard's bottom line: Call on the power and presence of Christ when forgiveness is needed. Let Christ do the forgiving in and through us.

Session 3

Health Benefits

Study Guide

1. Begin with a few moments of silence, followed with prayer. Silence can be helpful each time you begin your group meetings. Silence has a way of facilitating relaxation and focusing. Receive input from the group members on their feelings about starting each meeting with a brief time of silence.

2. Invite comments on Harry Camp's "Seven-Step Process Of Forgiveness." Did anyone try this at home? Share some personal experiences.

3. Turn to "Health Benefits." Notice the two columns related to unforgiveness and forgiveness. Have the group members check-off those emotions and feelings they have experienced in their personal situations. Do this silently. Then invite comments from the group.

4. Several studies are cited that reinforce the positive relationship between forgiveness and health. Ask the group members to think about specific instances in their own lives when unforgiveness seemed to cause unhealthy spin-offs and when forgiveness appeared to be a positive factor in restoring or improving health (physically, spiritually, mentally, and emotionally).

5. Unconfessed sin and lingering guilt have a negative impact on personal health. Discuss Dr. Dale Matthews' statement on page 44.

6. Turn to "Three Principles Of Forgiveness." Dr. Anderson Spickard is convinced that within those who have alcohol and drug abuse habits, forgiveness is a universal need and guilt is a universal fact. Discuss his three forgiveness principles:

   • Forgive Others
   • Forgive God
   • Forgive Self

7. Can these principles be applied in other circumstances? Be specific.

8. What are some ways that forgiveness can be a form of healing?

9. Closure: The leader will guide the group in this visualization prayer. Turn once more to the two columns of emotions and feelings related to unforgiveness and forgiveness. In silence picture yourself standing between the two lists. Which column comes closer to reflecting your personal lifestyle and/or your present situation? Where in your life and with whom do you need divine assistance? Open your heart and spirit to the heart and spirit of Christ. Be willing to pray, to do, to become a forgiver whenever and wherever forgiveness is absent. Take your time. Be sincere. Pray as you are able, not as others might have you pray. Thank God for this special time and commit yourself, with God's help, to continue what you began today.

10. Homework: Study "Reconciliation Scenarios" in Session 4. Do the "A Guide For Private Prayers Of Forgiveness" (prayer exercise).

Reconciliation

Those who cannot forgive others break the bridge over which they must pass, for everyone has need to be forgiven. — Lord Herbert

Reconcile ... to restore; to agree; to make good again.

Reconciliation ... a bringing together again in friendship or harmony; a mutual settlement of disagreements.

Reconciliation is the ideal solution or resolution to estranged and strained relationships. Yet this goal too often goes unrealized. The result is frustration, discouragement, anger, and guilt. When reconciliation is not achieved, after trying very hard, many of us take it personally. Somewhere along the way we have been taught, or have come to believe that unless every broken relationship is patched up, reconciled, and made good again there is something wrong with the one who is making the attempt to improve the situation. Reconciliation is a worthy, but not always achievable, goal. The key word in any reconciling action is mutuality. It takes two to reconcile. If only one party is interested in getting together again, reconciliation is totally unrealistic. The feelings, the forgiveness, the desire to change the relationship must be mutual. Even Jesus knew that not every attempt to reconcile would be successful. Here is a step-by-step strategy endorsed by Jesus in dealing with relationship problems within the body of believers, the church.

> *[Jesus said] If another member of the church sins against you, go and point out the fault when the two of you are alone. If the member listens to you, you have regained that one. But if you are not listened to, take one or two others along with you, so that every word*

may be confirmed by the evidence of two or three wit-
nesses. If the member refuses to listen to them, tell it to
the whole church; and if the offender refuses to listen
even to the church, let such a one be to you as a Gentile
and a tax collector. — Matthew 18:15-17

We must be careful not to interpret the last option as condemning forever the unrepentant one. Eugene H. Peterson, in his contemporary rendering of the New Testament, The Message, offers
this translation of Matthew 15:17:

If he won't listen to the church, you'll have to start over
from scratch, confront him with the need for repentance,
and offer again God's forgiving love.

Jesus does not give his followers the option of "writing off"
anyone forever and ever, but he is clear that we have no control
over anyone except ourselves. We can apologize, counsel, forgive,
love, and pray, but we cannot force or coerce another human being
into a reconciled relationship. Again, mutuality is the key.

Christians often find themselves in the middle of broken relationships, with a heartfelt desire to help in some way. After all, the
scriptures are clear at this point.

All this is from God, who reconciled us to himself
through Christ, and has given us the ministry of recon-
ciliation; that is, in Christ God was reconciling the
world to himself, not counting their trespasses against
them, and entrusting the message of reconciliation to
us. So we are ambassadors for Christ, since God is
making his appeal through us; we entreat you on be-
half of Christ, be reconciled to God.
— 2 Corinthians 5:18-20

The primary relationship that needs to be reconciled, according to the apostle Paul, is our relationship with God. In and through
and with Christ, God is constantly at work in our world offering to
welcome home wayward and sinful human beings. Furthermore,

God has given to the church, the body of Christ, the ongoing ministry of reconciliation. As the scripture says: "We are ambassadors for Christ, since God is making his appeal through us."

Compassionate, sensitive, caring Christians throughout the ages, and continuing to this moment, have been moved, not only to invite whomever will to accept Christ and be reconciled to God, but also to be instruments of reconciliation between two human beings, attempting to restore harmonious relationships. Although this is risky, it is the right thing to do, or at least to attempt, knowing that reconciliation efforts are never "a done deal." Human free will always has the option of accepting or rejecting the love of God, as well as the forgiving overtures from other people.

Marjorie J. Thompson, an ordained minister in the Presbyterian Church USA, retreat leader, and author of several excellent Christian formation resources, helps us further clarify the significance of reconciliation in the forgiveness process. Ponder her distinction between one-way and two-way forgiveness.

One-Way Forgiveness

This is a matter of releasing others from the judgment in my own heart. Such unilateral forgiveness does more than release me from the corrosive burden of anger and bitterness that eats away my peace of soul, although this is certainly one of the great gifts inherent in forgiveness. Moreover, I believe that hidden forgiveness affects the spirit of the person who has been released in ways that go beyond our comprehension or perception. I can forgive a friend who doesn't know she has hurt me; I can forgive a parent or grandparent who is no longer present on this earth; I can forgive people or groups of people without their consciously knowing it or having any way to respond.

Two-Way Forgiveness

Reconciliation is a two-way street ... the promise that lies at the heart of forgiveness; it is the full flower of the seed of forgiveness, even when that seed is hidden from sight. The gift of forgiveness will always feel incomplete if it does not bear fruit in reconciliation. This, I am convinced, holds as true in God's forgiveness of us as it does in our forgiveness of one another. Reconciliation means full restoration of a whole relationship, and as such requires conscious mutuality. No reconciliation can take place unless the offender recognizes the offense, desires to be forgiven, and is willing to receive forgiveness.[26]

Actually, when one consciously remembers that forgiveness in any form or category always begins in the heart of God, it might be more accurate to speak of one-way, two-way, and three-way forgiveness.

- **One-Way Forgiveness:** God's eternal love and forgiveness go out non-stop to all people, even before they are born.

   "God proves his love for us in that while we still were sinners Christ died for us." — Romans 5:8

   "God did not send the Son into the world to condemn the world, but in order that the world might be saved through him." — John 3:17

- **Two-Way Forgiveness:** Acknowledging with deep gratitude God's forgiveness of us, we take the initiative in forgiving and releasing those who have offended or hurt us in any way.
- **Three-Way Forgiveness:** God's active grace and mercy in my life motivate me to attempt to restore a broken relationship. When the other person responds with an affirming, forgiving attitude, reconciliation is achieved.

Marjorie Thompson writes about Bishop Donald Tippett who was in his office one day when two young men dropped in, hoping to establish an alibi for their planned robbery. When the bishop took a phone call in another room, the young men feared he had sized them up and was about to report them. They attacked him with brass knuckles, doing permanent damage to his left eye. When the two men came to trial, Tippett pleaded for a reduced sentence. He visited them regularly in prison. After the young men were

52

released, the bishop helped one of them financially to further his education and eventually saw him become (of all things) an ophthalmologist.

Tippett expressed his forgiveness of these men by persevering in returning good for evil. Yet, in his realistic love for them, he did not object to their reduced prison sentence. These young men had much to learn; and while learning, they needed to be prevented from doing further harm. They received due punishment under the law even though their victim personally forgave and helped them. Bishop Tippett actively sought reconciliation with his two attackers, and the benefits eventually became abundantly apparent.[27]

Marjorie Thompson is convinced that this story points us to the sacred ground of forgiveness.

> *Our forgiving is rooted in God's forgiveness of us. Because we know ourselves to be forgiven, we too can forgive. God is in the business of creating a new future out of our mistakes and bad decisions, out of our wounds and woundings.*[28]

A Guide For Private Prayers Of Forgiveness

In the quiet of your room or your favorite devotional spot, take some unhurried time to ponder these thoughts:

- When someone hurts me or fails to meet my expectations, am I able to forgive him or her immediately without harboring a grudge and without frequently rehearsing my grievance in my mind? *(pause)*
- If the answer is "No," in what ways does my resentment work itself out in my life and in my attitude toward that person? How do I feel about that person?
- How do I feel about myself? *(do not rush)*

Next make a list of individuals you cannot stand to be around:

- who have been unkind to you.
- who go out of their way to hurt you.

- who insist on their own way.
- who do not listen to you.
- who constantly try to change you.
- who put you down.

Then check out how you feel about yourself. In what areas do you need to forgive yourself?

What about your relationship with God?

- In what ways are you upset or angry with God?
- In what ways do you feel God has let you down?

When you are ready, ask God, in your own sincere way, to forgive you and to cleanse you of all resentment and hurt feelings. As the love begins to flow from God to you and from you to God, ask God to fill you with peace and joy. *(do not rush)*

Return to your list of individuals, lifting up each one by name into the light and love of the healing, forgiving Christ. Intentionally forgive each one, just as God through Christ forgives you. *(take your time)*

Then offer your personal prayer of thanksgiving to God for the gift of forgiveness and for this opportunity to give this gift to others. Amen.[29]

Unison Prayer

We thank you, merciful God, for giving each of us the gift of forgiveness at various times in our lives. Empower us and motivate us to give to others the gift of forgiveness, in the blessed name of Jesus we pray. Amen.

Reconciliation

Study Guide

1. Begin with silence and prayer.

2. Review the definitions of "reconcile" and "reconciliation."

3. Question: Has anyone in the group had the experience of being reconciled with another person? If so, invite that person to
   describe the circumstances and how the reconciliation was
   achieved.

4. Question: Has anyone in the group had the experience of attempting reconciliation but not achieving reconciliation? If so,
   invite that person to share some of the details and difficulties
   encountered.

5. Discuss Marjorie Thompson's distinction between one-way and
   two-way forgiveness. Then consider the author's statement that
   "forgiveness in any form or category always begins in the heart
   of God. It might be more accurate to speak of one-way, two-
   way, and three-way forgiveness."

6. Closure: Turn to "A Guide For Private Prayers Of Forgiveness."
   You were asked to make a list of those persons who have been
   unkind to you, who go out of their way to hurt you, who insist
   on their own way, who do not listen to you, who constantly try
   to change you, or who put you down.

       Return to your list, lifting up each one by name into the
   light and love of the healing, forgiving Christ. Intentionally

forgive each one, just as God through Christ forgives you. *(pause)* If you are not ready or unwilling to forgive some of the people on your list, sincerely ask God to help you to be willing some day to forgive. *(pause)*

Read the Unison Prayer on page 54.

7. Homework: Pray for one another and study "The Forgiveness Clause In The Lord's Prayer" in Session 5.

Matthew 6:12; Luke 11:4

Session 5

The Forgiveness Clause
In The Lord's Prayer

*For it is in giving that we receive; it is in pardoning
that we are pardoned.* — Saint Francis of Assisi

The prayer most prayed in all of Christendom, the prayer whose majestic poetry inspires believers of every Christian tradition, the one prayer pattern that Jesus taught his students is reverently lifted to God countless numbers of times every day throughout the world. Commonly called the "Lord's Prayer," it is recorded in two versions: Matthew 6:9-13 and Luke 11:2-4.

Christians would have an easier time praying this prayer if Jesus had only left out one line. Of the six petitions in the Lord's Prayer, this one is the most difficult to comprehend and to practice.

*And forgive us our debts, as we also have forgiven our
debtors.* — Matthew 6:12

*And forgive us our sins, for we ourselves forgive every-
one indebted to us.* — Luke 11:4

Chrysostom, an early church leader, wrote that in his day there were many Christians who suppressed this clause in the Lord's Prayer altogether.[30] This particular petition would be more acceptable if Jesus had only changed a word or two, such as: "Forgive us our sins, even though we have problems forgiving others." Or possibly, "Forgive us our debts, and help us do a better job of forgiving our debtors."

Another rewording might be "Thanks for forgiving us, but please overlook our unforgiving attitude toward certain people."

57

Another source of confusion that exists in the minds of some Christians is the exact wording of the "forgiveness clause." In Matthew 6:12 the Greek words for "debts" and "debtors" can also be translated "sins" or "trespasses." Consequently, English translators have several ways to communicate the original Greek. Is one way more correct than another? Not at all.[31]

William Barclay, the noted Scottish New Testament scholar, adds another interpretive level when he writes: "Of all petitions of the Lord's Prayer this is the most frightening." He goes on to point out that "Forgive us our debts as we forgive our debtors" has this literal meaning: "Forgive us our sins in proportion as we forgive those who have sinned against us."[32] Then we must deal with the footnote Jesus added:

> *For if you forgive others their trespasses, your heavenly Father will also forgive you; but if you do not forgive others, neither will your Father forgive your trespasses.* — Matthew 6:14-15

If we forgive others, God will forgive us. If we do not forgive others, God will not forgive us. Barclay's interpretation goes like this: "It is quite clear that, if we pray this petition with an unhealed breach, an unsettled quarrel in our lives, we are asking God not to forgive us."[33]

He underscores the seriousness of this petition with a story from the life of author Robert Louis Stevenson, who in his later years conducted daily family devotions. One morning in the middle of the Lord's Prayer he rose from his knees and left the room. His health was always precarious, and his wife followed him thinking that he was ill. "Is there anything wrong?" she asked. "Only this," said Stevenson, "I am not fit to pray the Lord's prayer today."[34]

Obviously, Jesus wanted to teach us that there is the closest possible connection between human and divine forgiveness. You can't have one without the other. Let us also be aware that this is a key spiritual principle as frequently taught and lived by Jesus. Check out these other scriptures:

Do not judge, and you will not be judged; do not condemn, and you will not be condemned. Forgive, and you will be forgiven. — Luke 6:37

Whenever you stand praying, forgive, if you have anything against anyone; so that your Father in heaven may also forgive you your trespasses. But if you do not forgive, neither will your Father in heaven forgive your trespasses. — Mark 11:25-26

Some may argue that this comes close to bargaining with God. If I do this, then God is obligated to do that. If I forgive everyone I know who has anything against me, then God has no choice but to welcome me into God's circle of the forgiven ones.

Is Jesus suggesting that we play "Let's make a deal with God"? Of course not. Rather, Jesus is using strong language urging his followers to be consistent in their everyday living patterns. What appears to be a tough teaching of Jesus is quite logical.

- How can you pray to God asking for world peace if you are not a peacemaker in your own church and community?
- How can you ask God to resolve family problems if you persist in behaving badly at home?
- How can you seek divine help in solving your money problems if you mismanage the financial resources you already have?
- How can you ask God to heal your sickness if you are not willing to work at achieving healthier living patterns?
- How can you expect God to forgive you if you are unwilling to forgive others or if you are unwilling to try to be a forgiving person?

Let us not take the "forgiveness clause" in the Lord's Prayer out of context. Jesus is clearly and boldly insisting on consistency and faithfulness in following him and in day-to-day living out his teachings. Furthermore, let us affirm and celebrate God's consistency, initiative, and unlimited love.

A wise pastor once said that one must be very careful about emphasizing one verse of scripture as the absolute truth, no questions asked. The Bible in all its God-given wisdom presents a balanced theology. When a particular passage seems to defy human understanding, explore other parts of the Bible to enlighten and explain. Here is only a sampling of the biblical teachings that remind us of God's unlimited grace and initiating attitude of forgiveness.

Because the Lord is like a loving shepherd, I have everything I need.   — Psalm 23:1 (TLB)

For God so loved the world that he gave his only Son, so that everyone who believes in him may not perish but may have eternal life.   — John 3:16

I came that they may have life and have it abundantly. I am the good shepherd.   — John 10:10-11

God did not send the Son into the world to condemn the world, but in order that the world might be saved through him.   — John 3:17

The Lord is merciful and gracious, slow to anger and abounding in steadfast love. As far as the east is from the west, so far the Lord removes our transgressions (sins) from us.   — Psalm 103:8, 12

God proves his love for us in that while we still were sinners Christ died for us.   — Romans 5:8

There is, therefore, now no condemnation for those who are in Christ Jesus.   — Romans 8:1

Do not worry about anything, but in everything by prayer and supplication with thanksgiving let your requests be made known to God. And the peace of God, which surpasses all understanding, will guard your hearts and your minds in Christ Jesus.
     — Philippians 4:6-7

Let us love one another because love is from God; God is love. God's love was revealed among us in this way: God sent his only Son into the world so that we might live through him ... if we love one another, God lives in us, and his love is perfected in us.

— 1 John 4:7-9, 12

God has acted, and continues to act, on our behalf. The Christian response is to act in ways that are pleasing to God and are faithful to God's Son, Jesus, our Lord and Savior. Consequently, if we do not forgive others, as God has already forgiven us, we are creating unnecessary impediments in our ongoing relationship with God. When we intentionally withhold forgiveness, we are intentionally denying, ignoring, and rejecting God's forgiveness of us. Each time we pray the Lord's Prayer, we are reminded of inconsistencies in our personal relationships and we are asking God to help us be more consistent in treating others the way God treats us. The "forgiveness clause" in the Lord's Prayer is an example of an all-encompassing teaching of Jesus: "Be perfect, therefore, as your heavenly Father is perfect" (Matthew 5:48).

Reminding us that humankind is created in the image of God, Barclay comments:

The great characteristic of God is love to saint and to sinner alike. No matter what [they] do ... God seeks nothing but their highest good. It is the whole teaching of the Bible that we realize our [humanity] only by becoming godlike. The one thing which makes us like God is the love which never ceases to care for [us], no matter what. We realize our [humanity], we enter upon Christian perfection, when we learn to forgive as God forgives, and to love as God loves.[35]

The following story illustrates the help, healing, and hope available to those who apply the "forgiveness clause" in their personal situations. A misunderstanding had bitterly estranged two sisters. The one who told this story confessed that her resentment darkened through the passing years and something beautiful died within.

61

She was not only hurting her sister, she was injuring herself. Then on a Sunday, words of scripture in the worship liturgy took hold of her mind and heart: "For if you forgive others their trespasses, your heavenly Father will also forgive you; but if you do not forgive others, neither will your Father forgive your trespasses" (Matthew 6:14-15).

That afternoon she wrote a letter to her sister, a letter that breathed love, forgiveness, and reconciliation. She said, "When I dropped that letter into the mailbox, it was like a thousand 'alleluias' singing inside me. The world was beautiful again and I felt alive for the first time in years."[36]

The Jesus way of forgiveness is down to earth, powerful therapy, with positive results. Charles L. Allen has an excellent suggestion when praying the "forgiveness clause" in the Lord's Prayer:

> *One of the most helpful experiences in prayer is to sub-stitute the name of a particular person in the petition: "Forgive me as I forgive _____."*
>
> *As I pray this prayer, a name comes before me. [I] keep praying until that name is clear in my own mind and in my own heart.*[37]

Paul's letter to the Colossians highlights again the necessity of developing a forgiveness lifestyle following the Jesus paradigm:

> *Bear with one another and, if anyone has a complaint against another, forgive each other; just as the Lord has forgiven you, so you also must forgive.*
> — Colossians 3:13

Rather than skipping lightly over the "forgiveness clause" or trying to ignore its clear intention, Jesus desires his followers to be consistent and constant, not only in receiving God's merciful forgiveness, but also in giving to others this same gracious gift.

Forgiving Others

Author's Note: An ordained minister in the Presbyterian Church USA, Marjorie J. Thompson is the Director of the Pathways Center for Spiritual Leadership with The Upper Room Ministries in Nashville, Tennessee. She has played a central role in developing the spiritual formation series, "Companions in Christ." The following is from her book, *The Way Of Forgiveness.*

> *Forgiveness is God's most astonishing response to human sin. It is the only response that could give hope for a new life. That same hope enables us to envision a new future in our relationships with others who have wounded us or offended us ... It is the emotional side of human life that makes forgiveness difficult. Even a strong appreciation of what God has done for us in Christ does not translate easily into forgiving others.*

> *Those who practice the grace-full art of forgiveness know increasing joy and freedom in their relationships. Forgiveness is one of the eminent signs of the vitality of the Holy Spirit in our midst. The Spirit ever plays the flute within, inviting us to dance to its tune. The Spirit keeps nudging the image of God hid deep in the soul, reshaping it to look more like the one who fashioned it. The Spirit breathes possibility into impossibility and authorizes us to forgive as God forgives. Through the Holy Spirit we abide in Christ and Christ in us. What privilege, what gift!*

I recommend Marjorie Thompson's three forgiveness exercises that you can do in the privacy of your own time and space. Keep a notebook close by to record your insights, questions, and reflections. Remember that you cannot force yourself to forgive, since that would not be authentic. Yet you can accept the challenge to move forward from an unforgiving spirit to a new place of mind and heart that may prepare you better to forgive.

Exercise 1 — Read Matthew 6:9-15

Jesus' strong emphasis on forgiveness in the Lord's Prayer and elsewhere calls us to be pragmatic in assessing "our debtors" in the spirit as in our financial relationships. Make a "forgiveness list." Include all the debtors you can think of, all those people you feel owe you something — an apology, compensation, their reputation, or their very life — for the way they hurt you or someone you love. Beside each name, note what you think he or she owes you. Return to the Lord's Prayer. Dwell on the promise that God will "forgive us our debts, as we also have forgiven our debtors." Weigh the options before you: "a pound of flesh" from your debtors or God's peace in your heart. Begin the process of forgiving by praying for the desire to forgive in each case. Keep a record of your progress.

Exercise 2 — Read Acts 9:10-19

In this story the Lord sends Ananias to lay the hands of Christ's love on Saul, a man infamous for persecuting Christians. Ananias' resistance is rooted in a forgiveness issue: whether or not to risk following the Lord's leading in reaching out with love to an enemy. Ananias, it seems, forgives more for the sake of the Lord than for himself, yet thereby makes way for the unfolding work of God. What unlikely soul is the Lord prompting you to reach out to, perhaps not so much for your sake as for Christ's? Pray your honest reactions just as Ananias did, and listen for the Lord's guidance. Remember the inexhaustible gift of grace God has bestowed upon you, which God invites you daily to pass on to another. Record your reflections.

Exercise 3 — Read Luke 23:34-43

Dwell on Jesus' prayer of pardon from the cross for those who crucified him (and for one of the thieves crucified with him). We hear and receive in these words the good news of God's pardon for sin. Extend the circle of grace now by praying these words while keeping before you the names of those you need to forgive. As you pray, consider what Jesus meant by the words, "They do not know what they are doing," when by all appearances on a human level they knew perfectly well. Allow yourself by the grace of the Spirit to enter into the forgiving mind of Christ for those who concern you. Record your learning from inside the mind of Christ.

If you feel ready, write a letter of forgiveness to one of the persons on your debtor list.

Writing A Letter Of Forgiveness

Write a letter of forgiveness to someone toward whom you feel resentment.

It could be someone who has already died, or whom you'll never see again. Perhaps it is someone you live or work with. It could be yourself. Who needs forgiveness from you? Write to that person.

First, acknowledge the truth of your negative feelings — all your hurt and anger, your pain and grief. Be absolutely honest.

Then release it. Let go of the burden of your resentment, anger, anguish, and guilt for feeling these things. Confirm that you are doing this in your writing.

Let the matter lie where it will with respect to the other person; you cannot be responsible for his or her feelings or responses, only your own. You are choosing to free yourself from this particular bondage to the past.

Remember that God has empowered you to forgive, once and for all, on the cross. Ask for the grace to let God take the burden from you, now and forever. You may decide at some point to send this letter, or you may not. Regardless, you can expect healing and new energy to flow from this exercise in faith.

The Forgiveness Paradigm Of Jesus

Without forgiveness there is no future.
— Archbishop Desmond Tutu

The Jesus way of forgiveness is unparalleled when compared to non-Christian religions. In Buddhism, forgiveness is an implied component in the practice of forbearance and compassion. Likewise, in Hinduism, forgiveness is important, but not a foundational teaching.

This is not the case in Islam, Judaism, and Christianity. These religions, all three tracing their roots to Abraham, believe in one God and teach their followers to imitate God, who is merciful and forgiving by nature. However, upon closer examination of the forgiveness writings and practices of these three faith traditions, the Jesus model is quite unique.[38]

Consider the Jesus paradigm for your life and your world. Paradigm comes from the Latin word *paradigma* meaning to show or point out something by comparison. A paradigm can be an example, a pattern, a standard, or a model. The Jesus way of forgiveness challenges our basic nature and offers alternate responses. Reflect on these comparisons.

Human Nature	**The Jesus Paradigm**
Seeks revenge by striking back. "An eye for an eye, a tooth for a tooth" (Matthew 5:38).	Does not strike back. "Love your enemies and pray for those who harm you" (Matthew 5:44).
Hates those who persecute you.	Blesses those who hurt you.
Holds grudges.	Lets go of bitterness.
Offers no second chance.	Offers repeated opportunities to start over.
Keeps a record of wrongs.	Keeps no score.

Focuses on the negative.	Focuses on the positive.
Lives in the past; keeps painful memories alive.	Lives in the present; has hope for the future.
Does not attempt reconciliation.	Attempts reconciliation.
Sees forgiveness as a weakness.	Sees forgiveness as a strength.
Does not offer an apology unless the other party goes first.	Offers an apology without waiting for the other party to go first.
Constantly criticizes others.	Makes an effort to examine and deal with personal faults and weaknesses.
Nurses a legalistic attitude with no mercy or grace.	Offers mercy and grace freely.
Refuses to explore peaceful solutions.	Tries to be a peacemaker.
Views forgiveness only as a remote possibility and waits for signs of repentance in the offender.	Understands the benefits of forgiveness and takes steps to initiate new beginnings.

To become better acquainted with the Jesus paradigm, we will explore eight biblical passages that give us knowledge, insight, and understanding about forgiveness. Sometimes the Bible is compared to a watermelon. The best way to determine the ripeness of a watermelon is to insert a sharp knife deep inside and remove a portion of the fruit. Taking a small plug from any area of the watermelon gives a true reading on what is inside. Likewise, "taking a plug" from any portion of the Bible gives an accurate sampling of what is inside: namely, story after story of God's willingness to love and forgive, of God's expectations of people to be loving and forgiving, and of God's grace and mercy available to all who desire to be more loving and forgiving.

You are invited now to open your Bible. Take several "plugs" from the four gospels. Sample the fruit from the vine of God's Word. Taste and see that the Jesus paradigm is the proven path to being forgiven and forgiving.

Session 5

The Forgiveness Clause In The Lord's Prayer

Study Guide

1. Begin with silence. Then all pray in unison the Lord's Prayer directly from Matthew 6:9-13. It is not necessary for all to read from the same English translation. The traditional doxology added at the end is not in Matthew's gospel; however, it is quite appropriate and consistent with the teaching of Jesus in his model prayer: "For thine is the kingdom, the power and the glory forever and ever. Amen."

2. Turn to "The Forgiveness Paradigm Of Jesus." Look at the fifteen comparisons noted in two columns showing the contrasts between human nature and the Jesus paradigm of forgiveness. Divide the group in half. Group A will read the characteristics of human nature and Group B will respond with the Jesus model. To illustrate: Group A "Human nature seeks revenge by striking back." Group B "The Jesus Paradigm does not strike back." Read all fifteen, line by line. When finished, ask for comments from the group.

3. Turn to "The Forgiveness Clause In The Lord's Prayer." Discuss these statements taken from the text:

   • Christians would have an easier time praying this prayer if Jesus had only left out one line: "Forgive us ... as we forgive ..." (Matthew 6:12).
   • William Barclay writes that the literal translation from the Greek is: "Forgive us our sins in proportion as we forgive those who have sinned against us."[29]

- Read Matthew 6:14-15. Barclay declares that this "footnote" by Jesus implies: "We are asking God not to forgive us, when we pray this prayer with unforgiveness in our hearts and minds toward another human being."
- Some may argue that this comes close to bargaining with God. If I do this then God is obligated to do that ... Is Jesus suggesting that we play "Let's make a deal with God"?

4. Ask the group members to share their interpretation of the "Forgiveness Clause."

5. Discuss the author's commentary.

6. Closure: Turn to "Forgiving Others" on page 63. Marjorie Thompson offers three personal forgiveness exercises based on three scripture teachings: Matthew 6:9-15; Acts 9:10-19; and Luke 23:34-43. Each group member is urged to do these at home, taking as much time as needed. At the end of this session is a suggested format for "Writing A Letter Of Forgiveness." During the last five minutes of the session, have everyone in the group begin to write a letter of forgiveness. Do this silently, finishing the letter at home. Participants may decide to send this letter, or not; however, each group member can expect healing grace and renewal to flow from this writing exercise. In closing pray once more, the Lord's Prayer.

7. Homework: Study "How Often Should I Forgive?" in Session 6.

Session 6

How Often Should I Forgive?

If we cannot love imperfect people, if we cannot for-
give them for their exasperating faults, we will con-
demn ourselves to a life of loneliness, because imper-
fect people are the only kind we will ever find.
— Harold S. Kushner

Contemporary Christians continue to be indebted to Peter, the spokesman for the twelve apostles of Jesus. Because of Peter's questioning mind, Jesus responded with some of his most memorable and practical teachings. Peter had been with Jesus from the start of his public ministry. Along with his brother, Andrew, Peter was among the first to be invited by Jesus to become a full-time disciple. Peter was present for the Sermon on the Mount. With his own ears he heard and received the instructions from Jesus:

- about the merciful people being blessed with mercy;
- about potential problems related to anger;
- about not seeking retaliation, but turning the other cheek; and
- about loving and praying for one's enemies.

Peter listened to Jesus outline a way of praying that glorified God and brought help to struggling people on earth. He had to be impressed that the so-called Disciples' Prayer or Lord's Prayer not only emphasized the connection between human and divine forgiveness, but also had an add-on line restating this spiritual principle:

For if you forgive others their trespasses, your heavenly
Father will also forgive you; but if you do not forgive
others, neither will your Father forgive your trespasses.
— Matthew 6:14-15

Yet Peter was bothered by something. Perhaps he was dealing with a nagging situation, possibly someone in the fellowship of Jesus who was constantly criticizing and making life miserable for him. Even though Peter knew Jesus' teachings on forgiveness, he wondered if forgiveness had limits and limitations. He decided to ask Jesus a question still raised by Christians today: "How often should I forgive?"

Who has not raised this question when someone repeatedly makes life difficult for us? The day that Peter raised this question with Jesus, he also suggested some forgiveness limits.

> *"Lord, if another member of the church sins against me, how often should I forgive? As many as seven times?" Jesus said to him, "Not seven times, but I tell you, seventy-seven times."* — Matthew 18:21-22

Lest we come down too hard on Peter, keep in mind that the Jewish forgiveness standard of that day was a maximum of three. Rabbinic teaching held that forgiveness did have limits. Rabbi Jose be Hanina said, "He who begs forgiveness from his neighbor must not do so more than three times."[39]

In suggesting as many as seven times, Peter thought he was going way beyond the norm. He not only doubled the limit of three, but added one more for a total of seven, expecting to be commended by Jesus. Peter's rationale could have been supported by a teaching of Jesus in the gospel of Luke.

> *If another disciple sins, you must rebuke the offender, and if there is repentance, you must forgive. And if the same person sins against you seven times a day, and turns back to you seven times and says, "I repent," you must forgive.* — Luke 17:3-4

However, if Peter was basing his forgiveness question and answer on this scripture, he totally missed Jesus' point. Peter took that teaching to mean that seven was an acceptable and quite generous number. Plus, repentance on the part of the offender was required. Jesus, however, is setting a new standard for forgiveness, not based on arithmetic and far exceeding traditional criteria. This is why Jesus intended his response of "seventy-seven times" to erase all thought of keeping score and setting limits on one's forgiveness patterns. To illustrate his principle of "forgiveness unlimited," the Master Teacher told Peter the parable of the unmerciful servant (Matthew 18:23-35).

Scene One: A servant owes his king an enormous amount of money, which he could never repay. Yet, in throwing himself on the king's mercy, something incredible happens. The king has pity, forgives the servant and releases him from the huge debt.

Scene Two: The debt-free servant then meets up with a fellow servant who owes him a small amount of money that could be repaid. However, when the second servant begs for patience, since he fully intended to repay the debt, the first servant mercilessly refuses and has the second servant thrown into prison.

Scene Three: Word gets back to the king who is furious. He calls in the first servant, gives him a lecture on forgiving others, even as this servant had been forgiven, revokes his pardon, and has the unmerciful servant imprisoned until the entire debt is repaid.

In the typical style of a mideastern storyteller, Jesus uses high drama, human interest, and contrasting details to communicate his message. Jesus makes his main point in answering Peter's original question in his conclusion to the parable:

> *So my heavenly Father will do to every one of you, if*
> *you do not forgive your brother or sister from the heart.*
> — Matthew 18:35

Notice there is no mention of a mathematical formula, rather acceptable forgiveness comes sincerely from one's heart without keeping score. Furthermore, Jesus would not want us to assume that the nature and character of God is an exact comparison to the king in the story. While on the one hand the king's desire to forgive excessive debt reminds us of God's forgiving attitude, on the other hand, God never revokes forgiveness nor imprisons debtors until all debts are paid in full. By our own unforgiving attitude and actions, we create our own prisons, locked in by our own selfishness.

Unwillingness on our part to forgive others is clear evidence that 1) we have not received and accepted God's forgiveness of us; or 2) we have received and are aware of God's forgiveness, but have not understood or accepted our role and responsibility to pass on to others God's mercy and grace. The unmerciful servant in this story gladly accepted the king's generous offer to erase (forgive) the huge money debt, but his heart and his attitude toward others was unchanged. The forgiven receiver refused to be a forgiveness giver. Here is a sad picture of a man who failed to follow through and who experienced the negative consequences of his own actions.

The Reverend Halford E. Luccock, a twentieth-century author, pastor, and teacher, goes so far as to say, "An unforgiving Christian is a contradiction in terms."[40]

Prayer Of Release And Prayer Of Blessing

Catherine Marshall, in her books, *Something More* and *Adventures in Prayer*, gives us several guidelines in dealing with difficult people and in forgiving what may seem to be unforgivable. In Mark 11:25, Jesus gives a clear, unconditional statement on forgiveness: "Forgive, if you have anything against anyone; so that your Father in heaven may also forgive you your trespasses." Helped by the insights of Christian friends and by seeking the guidance of the Holy Spirit, Catherine Marshall developed a new forgiveness pattern. She began by making lists of all those in her life who had ever hurt her in any way. Then she systematically lifted "anything and anyone" to God in what she called "Prayers of Release."

As she gave up the role of a critical judge passing condemnation on the wrongs of others, Catherine Marshall understood that "forgiveness is simply the decision of our wills to release a particular person, followed by verbalizing that to God. It can be a simple prayer like,

> *Lord Jesus, I release _____ from my judgment.*
> *Forgive me that I may have bound him (or her) and*
> *hampered your work by judging. Now I step out of the*

way so that heaven can go into action for _____.
Amen.

Obviously, there is nothing impossible about praying like that."[41]

Another helpful way to pray for those difficult ones who trouble you, often unmercifully, is called "The Prayer of Blessing." This also comes from Catherine Marshall as a nonjudgmental way of praying. Here is a sample Prayer of Blessing based on her guidelines:

> *Heavenly Father, I understand that you are love and joy and that you desire to make known your love and joy to everyone, even though no one is deserving, including myself. Therefore, I now release to you _____ from my judgment and I ask you to bless _____ abundantly in any and every way that seems good to you. Also, I ask that you so live within me that I shall desire as much good for others as I ask for myself and that I shall never again begrudge your blessings for others. Cleanse me of all selfishness and ungenerosity. Fill me with your joy and love, as you bless _____, whom I bless in your Holy Name. Amen.*[42]

To you, the reader: If you have never prayed prayers of releasing and prayers of blessing, try it. Pray sincerely and expectantly. As the official motto goes in a midwestern church:

> *Our role is to love people.*
> *God's role is to change people.*
> *Let us not confuse the two roles.*

Session 6

How Often Should I Forgive?

Study Guide

1. Begin with silence and prayer to center and focus.

2. Turn to "How Often Should I Forgive?" Ask one person to read Matthew 18:21-35 aloud.

3. Ask for reactions to Peter's question and to the parable that Jesus told in response to Peter's inquiry.

4. Test the group's memory: Can anyone recall a situation where someone repeatedly caused problems and heartache? How did you respond to the offender? Did you attempt to take evasive or positive action? Did you try to ignore the whole thing? Did you confront the offender? How is your relationship with this person today?

5. When you find yourself "keeping score" on a problem person, what are some ways you could begin to practice "forgiveness unlimited"?

6. Closure: Turn to the "Prayer Of Release And Prayer Of Blessing." Catherine Marshall's dilemma of withholding forgiveness until certain conditions were met was resolved by learning to pray simply and sincerely the Prayer of Release and the Prayer of Blessing. Discuss this section with the group. Then invite each one to name silently a difficult person in his or her life. The leader of the session will pray aloud "The Prayer Of Release And The Prayer Of Blessing," inviting each

group member to insert a name in the appropriate places in the prayers. After a few moments of silence say, "Amen."

7. Homework: Continue to pray these two prayers each day as a way of releasing, blessing, and forgiving. For the next session study "An Uninvited, Forgiven Guest" and "Forgiveness Training" from Session 7.

Session 7

An Uninvited, Forgiven Guest

I believe that genuinely forgiving people have certain
qualities that are born of suffering and for which they
have paid a high price. We learn to forgive as we learn
to love. — Paula Ripple

"Her sins, which were many, have been forgiven; hence, she has shown great love. But the one to whom little is forgiven, loves little," announced Jesus to Simon, his host at the interrupted dinner party. To fully understand this key forgiveness teaching, carefully read and reread the entire story as recorded in Luke 7:36-50. Revisit this tense drama spotlighting dehumanized community values versus the higher values of forgiveness and new beginnings.

One day, a community religious leader, Simon, invited the itinerant rabbi, Jesus, to his house for a meal. Other guests were present around the table. Why would Simon have opened his home to this select group? Perhaps he simply wanted his friends to have an opportunity to get to know Jesus firsthand, to discover for themselves why the popular support for this Galilean whose reputation preceded him wherever he went. Now mideastern hospitality dictated certain courtesies for invited guests. The host was expected to provide water and towels to wash and dry the dusty feet. Also a kiss of peace greeting and placing drops of sweet smelling perfume or ointment on the heads of the guests would be the customary order of the day. However, what we would assume happened when Jesus first entered Simon's house did not happen. This strange situation became even stranger when an unknown woman, an uninvited woman, a woman who remains nameless, but is identified as "a sinner," a woman with a shady reputation in the community, created quite a scene by humbly and boldly lavishing upon Jesus' feet the courtesies he had not received from Simon.

In those days, people would recline at low tables for meals leaning on one elbow, eating with the other hand, and extending their legs and feet away from the food, having previously removed their sandals. This explains how the woman could stand over Jesus' feet, wash them with her tears, dry them with her hair, kiss, and anoint them with perfume. All this, of course, infuriated Simon, whose socially correct gathering was totally disrupted by this woman of the street. Verse 39 informs us that Simon interpreted Jesus' acceptance of her actions as proof that Jesus was not from God, otherwise he would have known all about her sinful past and would not have allowed her to touch him. Jesus decided to confront Simon.

Notice what Jesus did not do. Jesus did not attempt a "quick fix" in an embarrassing circumstance. He did not say, "Simon, I know you don't understand what this woman is doing and I forgive you for not being a gracious host when I arrived here today. Can we just put this all aside and get on with the dinner?"

Apparently Jesus wanted to have Simon's full attention and addressed the issues somewhat indirectly, using two ways to help Simon understand what was really going on in those highly charged moments. First Jesus told Simon a brief parable about two men who owed another man sums of money. The one man had a debt amounting to 500 days' wages; the other man owed a sum of fifty days' wages. For some reason neither man could pay up, so the one to whom they were indebted canceled the debts for both.

"Simon," asked Jesus, "which man will love the creditor more?"

"I suppose," he answered, "the one who had the greater debt canceled."

"You have judged rightly," said Jesus.

Then to help Simon apply his acceptable answer to the immediate situation, Jesus turned to the woman, praising her for her non-verbal, but clear signs of appreciation and respect, unlike Simon's lack of common courtesies. Jesus proceeded to bring it all together by announcing to everyone in the room: "Furthermore, this dear woman, though her past sins were many, has been forgiven and has made a new beginning in her life. This is why she came here today, expressing her heartfelt gratitude."

Turning to Simon, Jesus continued, "But the one to whom little is forgiven, loves little." Or as Eugene H. Peterson translates this line in The Message: "If the forgiveness is minimal, the gratitude is minimal." Several learnings begin to emerge from this story of the uninvited, forgiven guest, demonstrating the Jesus way of forgiveness.

1. Jesus takes the initiative and does not wait for all involved parties to agree to be more agreeable. The woman was released from her sinful past, but the community still held her in bondage. Jesus attempted to unglue the community label of sinner.
2. Jesus confronts the issues, the hurt, the problem while attempting to rebuild and reconcile the relationships. He was assertive with Simon, but not condemning. He gave Simon opportunities to change his attitude and behavior. The story ends without informing us what Simon did or did not do.
3. Jesus offers total forgiveness with support and encouragement to start over, to begin anew without being stuck in the past. The dinner party ends with Jesus giving the woman a word of encouragement and affirmation: "Your faith has saved you; go in peace."

Whatever happened to this nameless, courageous soul we can only guess. She could well have been one of the women who accompanied Jesus and the twelve apostles, providing support and assistance "out of their resources" (Luke 8:1-3). However, she has blessed countless numbers of Christians with her example of unashamedly sharing her joy and gratitude to Jesus. She teaches us that people who have received the gift of forgiveness are inclined to be grateful, loving, and forgiving people. Question: Is the motivation to pass the gift of forgiveness on to others an automatic response? No, we always have a choice in the matter. Contrast the thankful woman's actions to the parable of the unmerciful servant in Matthew 18:21-35. Being forgiven a huge debt does not automatically instill the gift of generosity in our hearts. The self-centered servant was forgiven much but did not love much. He had a choice and chose wrongly. Simon had a choice in how poorly he treated Jesus, whom he had invited to be his guest and how insultingly he treated the uninvited woman. Did Simon have a positive change of heart after that unusual dinner party in his house? Or, did he hold on to his negative attitude and bitterness? He had a choice. We also have choices in how we treat other people.

Could we say that our desire to forgive others and our capacity to forgive others is directly connected with our personal experiences of being forgiven by God in Jesus Christ and by God's forgiving grace operating in and through other people? Thomas Merton, in his writings, says "Yes" to this question and affirms the Jesus way of forgiveness.

> *We do not really know how to forgive until we know what it is to be forgiven. Therefore, we should be glad that we can be forgiven by (others). It is our forgiveness of one another that makes the love of Jesus manifest in our lives, for in forgiving one another we act towards one another as He has acted toward us.*[43]

Forgiveness Training

Dr. Fred Luskin, Director and Cofounder of The Stanford University Forgiveness Project, has authored an easy-to-read, common sense approach, practical guide on the art and science of forgiveness. Taste this sampling from his excellent book *Forgive for Good*. Although Dr. Luskin does not write from a Christian perspective, his principles and techniques can easily be combined with the Jesus way of forgiveness.

What is forgiveness? In Dr. Luskin's words: "Forgiveness is the feeling of peace that emerges as you take your hurt less personally, take responsibility for how you feel, and become a hero instead of a victim in the story you tell. Forgiveness is the experience of peacefulness in the present moment. Forgiveness does not change the past, but it changes the present. Forgiveness means that even though you are wounded you choose to hurt and suffer less. Forgiveness means you become part of the solution. Forgiveness is the understanding that hurt is a normal part of life."[44]

"You forgive by challenging the rigid rules you have for other people's behavior and by focusing your attention on the good things in your life as opposed to the bad. Forgiveness does not mean forgetting or denying that painful things occurred. Forgiveness is the powerful assertion that bad things will not ruin your today even though they may have spoiled your past."[45]

Dr. Luskin continually emphasizes our choices in life and the control we have over ourselves, but not over others. He compares the human mind to a television screen. Just as we can choose to watch a wide variety of television channels, we can also tune our minds into a grievance, hurtful episode or switch to the forgiveness channel. Ask yourself, "What is playing on my set today?" Is your remote tuning into channels that will help you feel good?[46]

In his chapter on "Forgiveness Techniques For Healing," Dr. Luskin details and amplifies, step-by-step instructions, combined with real-life stories:

1. Changing the channel
2. Breath of thanks
3. Heart focus
4. PERT (Positive Emotion Refocusing Technique)

All of these are incorporated into his main method of forgiveness called HEAL (Hope, Educate, Affirm, Long-term). "Through the HEAL method you reduce the power of your grievance. You heal yourself, and you allow yourself to recover that loving, positive direction that lay behind much of your actions. The HEAL method is particularly useful whenever a disturbing memory or painful feeling emerges."

Guided Practice Of The HEAL Method (Brief Version)

At any time you feel hurt or anger over an unresolved grievance:

1. Bring your attention fully to your stomach as you slowly draw in and out two slow deep breaths.
2. On the third inhalation bring to your mind's eye an image of someone you love or of a beautiful scene in nature that fills you with awe and peace. Often people have a stronger response when they imagine their positive feelings are centered in the area around their heart. Continue to breathe slowly into and out of your belly.
3. Reflect on what you would have preferred to happen in this specific situation. Make a *Hope* statement that is personal, specific, and positive.
4. Then *Educate* yourself about the limitations in demanding things always work out the way you want.
5. *Affirm* your positive intention — the long-term goal underneath the hope you had for this specific grievance.
6. Make a *Long-term* commitment to practice the HEAL method and follow your positive intention.[47]

You may want to get a copy of this book and discover for yourself Dr. Luskin's ground-breaking research and proven methods in the forgiveness process.

Unison Prayer

God of grace and mercy, we thank you for the firm and wise ways that Jesus coped with unforgiving attitudes and behavior. Train us to be forgiving and faithful followers of your Son, our Savior, Jesus Christ. Amen.

Session 7

An Uninvited, Forgiven Guest

Study Guide

1. Begin with centering silence and prayer.

2. Discuss responses from praying the "Prayer Of Release And The Prayer Of Blessing" since the group last met.

3. Turn to "An Uninvited, Forgiven Guest." Ask someone to read Luke 7:36-50 to the group.

4. As you hear this story, what gets your attention? What causes you to want to stop the action of the story and ask a question or make a comment?

5. Using your imagination, picture yourself in Simon's house that day. Describe your feelings and emotions if you had been one of the invited dinner guests, or Simon, or the uninvited woman.

   Question: Are we guilty of keeping people glued to their sinful past? Conventional wisdom asks: "What would people think or say about us?"

   The Jesus way says: "Do the right thing. Human needs come first, not social customs."

6. Notice what Jesus did not do. Jesus did not attempt to "smooth over" an abrasive and potentially damaging scene. Actually Jesus took the occasion to present "Forgiveness Training" to Simon and his guests. In a nonaggressive way, Jesus told a short story to illustrate his point. Then he held up the woman's exemplary behavior, based on her forgiven past. Discuss the

three ways Jesus demonstrated forgiveness in Simon's house that day.

7. Discuss these related statements:
   • "The one to whom little is forgiven, loves little."
   • "We do not really know how to forgive until we know what it is to be forgiven."

8. Is it possible to be trained to forgive, to be taught certain helpful methods to use in the forgiveness process? Dr. Fred Luskin says it is. Turn to "Forgiveness Training." Discuss Dr. Luskin's definition of forgiveness.

9. Notice how Fred Luskin compares the human mind to a television screen. Just as we can choose to watch a wide variety of television channels, we can also tune into a grievance, a hurtful episode in our life, or we can switch to the forgiveness channel. Take a few moments to answer this question silently: "What is playing on my set today?"

10. In closing, invite all to pray the Unison Prayer on page 84.

11. Homework: Study "The Woman Accused Of Adultery" in Session 8.

Session 8

The Woman Accused Of Adultery

*One of the greatest blocks to healthy forgiveness is try-
ing to push too quickly past our emotional pain when
we have been hurt.* — Flora S. Wuellner

This next episode on forgiveness has several remarkable
characteristics:

- The entire scenario is a set-up. The woman accused of adultery is a pawn being used by some religious leaders to trap
  Jesus. (See Mark 3:1-6; Luke 10:25-28; Matthew 22:15-22.)
- Some biblical scholars question the authenticity of this story
  because it is not found in the oldest manuscripts of the New
  Testament. Consequently an inconsistency exists in English
  translations of this passage. Some place these eleven verses
  in a footnote to John 7; others locate the story at the beginning of John 8; and others simply leave it out of John's gospel, suggesting a more appropriate placement after Luke
  21:38.
- This story is consistent with the over-all ministry of Jesus
  and demonstrates his uncanny ability to turn potentially explosive situations into hard-hitting, teaching opportunities.
- This is one of the most dramatic, poignant, moving forgiveness stories in the Bible, yet the word "forgive" is not used.

Eugene H. Peterson's contemporary rendering of John 8:1-11
helps to draw us into the story and offers fresh understanding:

> *Jesus went across to Mount Olives, but he was soon
> back in the Temple again. Swarms of people came to*

87

him. He sat down and taught them. The religion schol-
ars and Pharisees led in a woman who had been caught
in an act of adultery. They stood her in plain sight of
everyone and said, "Teacher, this woman was caught
red-handed in the act of adultery. Moses, in the Law,
gives orders to stone such persons. What do you say?"
They were trying to trap him into saying something in-
criminating so they could bring charges against him.
Jesus bent down and wrote with his finger in the dirt.
They kept at him, badgering him. He straightened up
and said, "The sinless one among you, go first: Throw
the stone." Bending down again, he wrote some more
in the dirt. Hearing that, they walked away, one after
another, beginning with the oldest. The woman was left
alone. Jesus stood up and spoke to her. "Woman, where
are they? Does no one condemn you?" "No one, Mas-
ter." "Neither do I," said Jesus. "Go on your way. From
now on, don't sin."   — John 8:1-11 (The Message)

Let's focus first on the accusers, who were legally correct. The
Law of Moses was clear. A man and a woman who were married,
but not to each other, were strictly forbidden, under penalty of death,
to have sexual relations with one another (the sin of adultery).
However, the Hebrew scriptures were also quite definite that both
the man and the woman caught in an adulterous act were subject to
the death penalty. (See Leviticus 20:10; Deuteronomy 22:22.) So,
you ask, "Where is the guilty man in this alleged affair and why is
the accusing spotlight only on this disgraced, nameless woman?"

The answer lies in the malicious intent of the scribes and the
Pharisees that day. This all-male, self-appointed judge and jury
were intent, not on following to the letter the Law of Moses, but to
use this humiliated woman's situation as bate to lure Jesus into
entrapment. "Teacher, this woman was caught in the very act of
committing adultery. Now in the Law, Moses commanded us to
stone such women. Now what do you say?" (John 8:4-5).

If Jesus called for an immediate pardon, that could be interpreted as being too lenient toward adultery and not upholding the
Commandments of Moses. If Jesus agreed with the death sentence,

he would be labeled a criminal by the Roman authorities, who alone had the power to impose capital punishment on anyone, Jew and Gentile alike. Knowing their intent, Jesus acted quickly to diffuse and redirect the incriminating plot. Twice he bent down and, using a finger, inscribed something in the dirt. What he wrote has been the subject of much guess-work; however, what he said to the assembled accusers leaves no room for misinterpretation.

> *Let anyone among you who is without sin be the first to throw a stone at her.* — John 8:7

Was Jesus turning the tables and accusing the scribes and Pharisees of being adulterers? No! He takes a broader stroke by reminding them that all have sinned in one way or another. This is consistent with other teachings of Jesus:

> *Do not judge, so that you may not be judged.* — Matthew 7:1

> *Why do you see the speck in your neighbor's eye, but do not notice the log in your own eye?* — Matthew 7:3

> *You have heard that it was said, "You shall not commit adultery." But I say to you that everyone who looks at a woman with lust has already committed adultery with her in his heart.* — Matthew 5:27-28

Because no one is sinless, none could throw that first stone. This universal human condition was aptly illustrated one day when a young boy began to make fun of ole Joe, the town drunk. His wise mother took him aside and said, "Son, everyone in town knows ole Joe has problems and gets into trouble a lot. Don't be hard on ole Joe. The rest of us have problems and mess up also. The difference is that ole Joe's sins are so public, whereas the rest of us try to hide ours."

Jesus obviously touched a nerve in the consciences of his hearers. One by one they faded away, starting with the eldest in the group. Try to imagine the astonishment and amazement of the accused woman. What next? Was this Jesus about to condemn her, lecture her, preach at her or what? The two of them are now alone. Notice Jesus did not say: "Look, whatever-your-name-is, they had no right to treat you that way. You have suffered enough. Tell you what I'm going to do. If you will promise not to continue your adulterous ways, if you will try real hard to get your life back on the right track, I will let you go with my blessing. Okay?" No, that's not the Jesus way. The closing dialogue is much more challenging and forgiving than that.

> *"Woman, where are they? Has no one condemned you?"*
> *"No one, sir."*
> *"Neither do I condemn you. Go your way and from*
> *now on do not sin again."* — John 8:10-11

The Jesus way of forgiveness is bold, full of mercy, blotting out the entire deficit, and trusting the forgiven one to respond with a renewed sense of purpose and direction for starting over. A casual reading of this story could draw the wrong conclusion, that Jesus took this matter too lightly. Not at all. Although Jesus does not condemn her, neither does he excuse her behavior. Instead, he releases her from her past and challenges her, encourages her, to become the kind of person God wants her to be.

William Barclay reminds us that in Jesus' conversation is unmistakably the gospel of another chance, the gospel of starting over. To paraphrase his words: "I know that you have made a mess of things; but life is not finished yet; I am giving you another chance, the chance to redeem yourself."[48] Jesus was always intensely interested, not only in what a person had been, but also in what a person could be. He did not say that what they had done did not matter; broken laws and broken hearts always matter; but Jesus was sure that everyone has a future as well as a past.

The woman in this story experienced firsthand the non-condemning, forgiving attitude of Jesus. For all who tend to engage in self-blame and self-condemnation, take to heart this spiritual truth from the apostle Paul:

90

There is therefore now no condemnation for those who
are in Christ Jesus. — Romans 8:1

The sensitive way that Jesus treated the accused woman is not an isolated case. In John 4:1-30, Jesus' conversation with the Samaritan woman at the well was neither condemning nor condoning. Instead Jesus used this opportunity to release her from the past, inspire her present, and offer her future possibilities.

Margaret G. Alter states in an article titled, "The Unnatural Act Of Forgiveness," published in *Christianity Today*, June 16, 1997, that Jesus, as he moves through the gospels, acts on two basic beliefs about human nature:

> ... *the universal need of forgiveness and the abiding presence of an interested and compassionate God. The radical nature of Jesus' relationship is that his forgiveness is not contingent upon our actions or attitudes. He doesn't ask for an apology — and, shockingly, he doesn't ask for repentance. Alter says, "It is as if the forgiveness precedes repentance; forgiveness itself creates safety for individuals to recognize how terribly alienated they are, how needy, how empty ... 'Go on your way, and from now on do not sin again,' Jesus says, empowering her to say no, to set boundaries."*[49]

We are grateful to John's gospel for including this dramatic and touching episode in the life and ministry of Jesus. However, this is an unfinished story. We are not told what happened after that or how the renewed and forgiven woman responded. If you are inclined to write your own ending, recall those grace-filled moments in your own life when you, indeed, experienced God's forgiveness and the chance to start over. How have you responded?

Session 8

The Woman Accused Of Adultery

Study Guide

1. Begin with centering silence and prayer.

2. Invite the group to listen closely as someone reads John 8:1-11.

3. Questions
    *   At what point in the story did you stop listening and begin to think about something related or something different?
    *   What questions would you like to ask the author of this gospel about this story?
    *   Can you make any connections in the story with life today?
    *   Other responses or comments?

4. Turn to "The Woman Accused Of Adultery." Invite group discussion around the commentaries by William Barclay and Margaret G. Alter.

5. Read John 8:1-11 aloud again, this time using Eugene H. Peterson's contemporary translation. This is an unfinished story. We are not told how the woman responded or what happened next in her life. Take a few minutes to write your own ending to this story, as you recall those grace-filled times in your own life when you experienced God's forgiveness and new beginnings.

6. Closure: In the sanctuary of your heart and with the ears of your inner spirit, hear, feel, and know these words of assurance addressed by Jesus to you: "_____, I do not

condemn you. Go your way. From now on, do not sin.""

7. Homework: Study "The Unforgivable Sin And Self-Forgive-
    ness" in Session 9. Invite three group members to be prepared
    in the next session to speak briefly on each of the three ap-
    proaches to self-forgiveness:

    _____ will report on Robert D. Jones.
    _____ will report on Thom Rutledge.
    _____ will report on William Thiele.

Session 9

The Unforgivable Sin
And Self-Forgiveness

Almost all our faults are more pardonable than the methods we think up to hide them. — Anonymous

Most of the forgiveness teachings of Jesus focus on other people, on improving human relationships, on the necessity of developing a compassionate, merciful lifestyle. However, the so-called "unforgivable sin" shifts our attention to one's relationship with God and the forbidden act called "blasphemy against the Holy Spirit."

"Truly I tell you," said Jesus, "people will be forgiven for their sins and whatever blasphemies they utter; but whoever blasphemes against the Holy Spirit can never have forgiveness, but is guilty of an eternal sin" (Mark 3:28-29). A hard passage to understand, these words of Jesus have prompted untold numbers of New Testament readers to ask: "Am I guilty of having committed the unforgivable sin?" In attempting to interpret this significant teaching, consider four questions:

1. What circumstances prompted Jesus to utter these daunting words?
2. What is the definition and meaning of blasphemy?
3. What else does the Bible say about issues related to this scripture?
4. What are some ways to apply this teaching of Jesus in our personal lives?

1. The context: Even though the settings surrounding these teachings are slightly different, the primary emphasis of Jesus is the same in all three versions. (See Matthew 12:31-32; Luke 12:10;

Mark 3:28-29.) Take a closer look at the context in Mark 3:19b-30. Here Jesus is being accused by certain religious leaders of healing people, not by the power of God, but rather by the power of Satan. Jesus, they said, is guilty of possessing an evil spirit within himself. This false charge, no doubt, upset Jesus who began to instruct them in parables about their unseemly logic saying, "How can Satan cast out Satan?"

The scribes, by labeling Jesus' good works as evil in nature, totally missed the point. The frustrated Jesus responds with words he might not have uttered under any other circumstance. To paraphrase Jesus: "Try to understand what I am about to say. You can be forgiven for all your sins and insults toward other people, but when you blaspheme against the Holy Spirit, then you have gone too far and have indeed committed an unpardonable sin."

The problem is that all too often, casual readers of the Bible take one sentence completely out of context and proceed to make that solo verse a universal truth, a lifelong mindset, a rationale for having the last word in any conversation that usually begins with: "Well, as it says in the Bible...." Surely you have heard people quote from the sacred scriptures putting their personal spin on the original meaning. Sadly, that has happened repeatedly with Jesus' teaching about the unforgivable sin. Some have tried to apply these words of Jesus to a variety of sinful situations. Whereas, Jesus was quite specific in declaring that blasphemy against the Holy Spirit is attributing the good works of God to Satan. But why did Jesus label this sin "unforgivable"?

2. Defining blasphemy: This English word, from the Greek *blasphemia*, has several meanings, all of them negative. A blasphemous person is irreverent, profane, impious, and sacrilegious. One who blasphemes exhibits a disrespectful attitude toward God or anything held in high esteem or deemed sacred by common consent. Cursing, desecrating, scoffing, swearing, and speaking evil are noticeable characteristics. Keep in mind that Jesus was called a blasphemer more than once by his adversaries. (See Matthew 9:3; Matthew 26:65; John 10:36.)

3. Related issues: As stated earlier, readers of the Bible can easily get sidetracked by basing their belief systems on a single passage; however, the Bible consistently corrects, edits, and brings understanding to what might first appear to be an error or an incompatible teaching. Such is the case with the biblical view of God's forgiving and merciful nature. To balance the concept of an unforgivable sin, ponder these passages:

> *The days are coming, says the Lord, when I will make a new covenant with the house of Israel and the house of Judah ... for I will forgive their iniquity, and remember their sin no more.* — Jeremiah 31:31, 34

> *For you, O Lord, are good and forgiving, abounding in steadfast love to all who call on you.* — Psalm 86:5

> *The Lord does not deal with us according to our sins. For as the heavens are high above the earth, so great is his steadfast love toward those who fear him; as far as the east is from the west, so far does the Lord remove our transgressions from us.* — Psalm 103:9-12

Question: How does one access and experience God's undeserved forgiveness and steadfast love?

Answer: If we confess our sins, [God] who is faithful and just will forgive us our sins and cleanse us from all unrighteousness (1 John 1:9).

In biblical language this is called "repentance" — having a change of heart, mind, and attitude. Repentance is the human desire and response, prompted by the Holy Spirit, to turn away from sin, to denounce the darkness of evil and to come to the light of forgiveness, health, and salvation in Jesus Christ. God's grace and mercy are always available, but we are not always receptive and willing to receive. To quote from the Interpreter's Dictionary of the Bible, "The unforgivable sin, blasphemy against the Holy Spirit, must be understood as the deliberate and perverse repudiation of God's saving work, whereby one consciously hardens (oneself) against repentance and the possibility of forgiveness."[50]

97

This is precisely the reason Jesus labels blasphemy against the Holy Spirit as "unforgivable." Those who choose to insult God, slander Jesus, and speak evil of the Holy Spirit's good works have chosen to cut themselves off from God who yearns to forgive and to remember their sins no more. The choice is theirs. The so-called "unforgivable sin" is not about God's reluctance to forgive, but more about human unwillingness to seek and accept God's forgiveness. As a wise seminary professor reassured his class one day, "The only sin God cannot forgive is the sin that remains unconfessed."

4. Applying this teaching of Jesus: Very few would actually blaspheme against the Holy Spirit or accuse Jesus of having anything to do with evil; yet, this particular teaching of Jesus has caused undue emotional distress among many devout Christians. Fearing that he had been guilty of this sin contributed to the recurring insanity of the English poet William Cowper.[51]

People who are unduly "distressed for fear that they may have committed the sin against the Holy Spirit should be told in most cases that their distress is proof enough that they have not committed that sin."[52]

Furthermore, if in fact they are guilty, then their restless consciences are leading them to repentance. To blaspheme God or to be blasphemous against God's Holy Spirit is the exact opposite of doing what Jesus taught us in the "Lord's Prayer," where we are instructed to make holy, to hold in highest regard, to show only honor and respectful reverence for God.

> *Our Father in heaven, hallowed be your name.*
> — Matthew 6:9

All who pray this prayer, with sincerity and genuine devotion, can never be guilty of committing the unforgivable sin. The third commandment of Moses also underscores the sacredness of God and God's name:

> *Thou shalt not take the name of the Lord thy God in vain.* — Exodus 20:7 (KJV)

98

To profane God's name, to swear and curse using God's name, is to reveal not only personal disrespect, but also an unhealthy relationship with God.

Eugene H. Peterson describes the essence of Jesus' teaching on the unforgivable sin in his unique paraphrase of Mark 3:28-29 in The Message:

> *"Listen carefully," said Jesus, "I'm warning you. There is nothing done or said that can't be forgiven. But if you persist in your slanders against the Holy Spirit, you are repudiating the very One who forgives, sawing off the branch on which you're sitting, severing by your own perversity all connection with the One who forgives." Jesus gave this warning because they were accusing him of being in league with Evil.*

Having defined the narrow scope and limits of the so-called unforgivable sin, sensitive human beings still have those occasions when God's forgiveness almost seems nowhere near of the realm of possibility.

The bottom line: The only sin God cannot forgive is the sin that remains unconfessed.

Self-Forgiveness

"You just have to forgive yourself."

"Let it go, forgive yourself, get on with your life."

"If you would forgive yourself, you would feel a lot better."

"I know I need to forgive myself, but how?"

Belief in the value of self-forgiveness is a popular concept among Christians and non-Christians alike. This notion that somehow, someway each of us is capable of forgiving one's self is silently and passively accepted, but difficult to do. Rarely are we given any guidelines on the process of self-forgiveness, other than, "just do it." Consider these three understandings of self-forgiveness. Each one approaches this illusive subject in a different way. Experiment with all three. Experience the way that works best for you.

1. *Forgiveness: I Just Can't Forgive Myself* (Phillipsburg, New Jersey: P&R Publishing Company, 2000), a booklet by Robert D. Jones, Pastor of Grace Fellowship Church of Culloden, West Virginia.

What does the Bible say about forgiving yourself? Surprisingly, nothing! You may study God's Word from cover to cover, but you will not find self-forgiveness mentioned, either by example or precept. The Bible speaks of vertical forgiveness (God forgiving a person) and horizontal forgiveness (one person forgiving another). Ephesians 4:32, for example, declares that God in Christ forgave us (vertical) and exhorts us to forgive others (horizontal). But the Bible says nothing of internal forgiveness (a person forgiving himself or herself). It is simply not taught in the scripture.

Pastor Jones suggests that the concept of self-forgiveness comes not from careful and prayerful study of the Bible, but from other sources, such as secular psychology and the felt needs of individual people. Yet, declares this Christian minister, there is a strong biblical alternative to the issue mislabled as an inability to forgive oneself. He lists five possibilities:

The Person Who Says, "I Just Can't Forgive Myself"
1. may simply be expressing an inability or unwillingness to grasp and receive God's forgiveness. This seems to be the most common explanation behind "self-forgiveness" talk. We say that we can't forgive ourselves because we really doubt that God has forgiven us.
2. may not see or be willing to acknowledge the depth of his/her own sinful nature. Inability to forgive oneself can be a form of pride, self-righteousness, and a lack of realistic self-knowledge.
3. may be venting his/her regrets for failing to achieve a certain cherished desire. In essence, such a person is saying, "I had an opportunity to get something I really wanted, but I threw it all away! I can't forgive myself." When desires are thwarted, the result is self-reproach and a haunting case of "if only I had...."
4. may be trying to establish his/her own standards of righteousness. "I can't forgive myself" could mean, "I haven't

lived up to my own perfect standards." But, the Bible tells us that God is the only one we must please; God's law must be our sole standard of self-measurement.

5. may have ascended to the throne of judgment and declared himself/herself to be his/her own judge. This is equivalent to saying, "I'm in the role of judge and will dispense forgiveness as I decide."

Robert Jones is convinced that the dilemma of self-forgiveness disappears when one accepts the grace, mercy, and forgiveness of Jesus Christ, as well as the trustworthy promises in the Bible. God has declared:

> *I have removed your sins as far as the east is from the west. Though they were like scarlet, I have made them white as snow. I have put all your sins behind my back. I, even I, am the One who blots out your transgressions, and remembers your sins no more. I have swept away your offenses like a cloud, your sins like the morning mist. I have tread them underfoot and hurled them into the ocean depths.*
> — (See Psalm 103:12; Isaiah 1:18; 38:17; 43:25; 44:22; Micah 7:19)

2. *The Self-Forgiveness Handbook*, by Dr. Thom Rutledge, a psychotherapist with a private practice in Nashville, Tennessee.

The author clearly states that "this is a book of psychology. For some readers this will quite naturally involve their spirituality, but there is no prerequisite belief system to benefit from *The Self-Forgiveness Handbook*. I encourage you to think of this as a guide to help you learn how to effectively receive forgiveness. What we are given from God or from each other, is of no use unless we can learn to accept the gift(s)."

This practical guide is built around seven components of self-forgiveness, with well-explained exercises on ways to incorporate these into your own situations. Liberally using stories and illustrations from his clients, Dr. Rutledge's humor, clarity, and compassion are evident throughout this handbook.

His understanding of forgiveness is based on what he calls self-compassion.

> *I believe that self-compassion is our first nature, and that excessive self-criticism and self-condemnation are a learned second nature. I believe that forgiveness of ourselves and others is not so much something we do, as it is that natural state when we are not holding on to old resentments, pain, and guilt. I also believe that resentments and grudges I hold against myself are every bit as destructive as those I harbor for the fellow down the street.*
>
> *I believe that living a life of self-compassion has nothing to do with being selfish, or in any way excluding others. I believe that the first step in giving is receiving; that when we are genuinely self-forgiving, the benefits automatically (or with minimal effort) will spill over into the lives of others. When we practice genuine self-forgiveness, we will naturally live according to a positive value system that includes respect for — and a desire for — the well being of others.*
>
> *I believe that in order to practice genuine self-forgiveness, we must accept full responsibility for who we are and what we do. Accountability is a requirement, and perfection is not an option. Finally, I believe that living a life of forgiveness, attending to daily life from the inside out, is the most energy efficient and most productive way to live. I believe that self-forgiveness is essentially inseparable from self-respect and self-responsibility.*

Dr. Thom Rutledge's *The Self-Forgiveness Handbook* (Oakland, California: New Harbinger Publishing, Inc., 1997), is highly recommended.

3. *The Process Of Self-Accepting-Forgiveness*, by Dr. William Thiele, a pastoral counselor in private practice in the New Orleans, Louisiana area.

> *One of the most common myths I have heard among Christians and non-Christians, is "You just have to*

forgive yourself." This puts a burden on the back of a guilty person. It says, "You have to do something for yourself that you cannot really do." Accidentally it may even come across as saying, "I don't really want to hear about your guilt." Perhaps this is never our intention, but telling a friend who is experiencing guilt that they need to "just get over it" relegates the person to suffer alone.

Let's be clear about this. You cannot forgive yourself by yourself. It is not possible! In fact Christian persons know that forgiveness comes from God, not from ourselves. But even if we believe this in our heads, in our bellies we often feel unforgiven. Guilt can linger for a long time.

Often guilt thoughts can return again and again. This does not mean we do not have "enough faith," as some preachers proclaim. Thoughts come because thoughts come. No person on this planet can control which thoughts come into his or her mind. No one has complete control of his or her own consciousness. So if we cannot forgive ourselves once and for all, if we cannot prevent guilt thoughts from coming to mind, what is a person to do?

Forgiveness is a process and self-forgiveness is a continuing necessity for those who decide not to allow the past to control the future or ruin the present. Dr. Thiele believes that forgiveness is a gift from God intended for all people and that God's compassion for each of us is not based on merit points or on what we deserve. God loves and accepts us even in our most guilty situations, our lowest states of mind, and in whatever circumstances we find ourselves. God's grace truly is amazing.

This means, then, that even though I cannot forgive myself I can accept God's gift of forgiveness repeatedly. In a way, the phrase "self-forgiveness" is a misnomer. The deeper truth and the more complete phrase is "self-accepting-forgiveness." Whenever I choose for myself to accept God's gracious, merciful forgiveness, I am engaging in "self-accepting-forgiveness."

Drawing from Christian tradition, as well as from his own experiences, Dr. Thiele names several resources that can be helpful in our personal quest for self-accepting-forgiveness:

1. Locate a spiritual director.
2. Meet with a pastoral counselor.
3. Have a soul friend.
4. Do personal journaling.
5. Pray our experience.
6. Visualize scripture scenes.

William Thiele goes on to share a deep conviction about the forgiveness process. "I emphasize the importance of speaking the desire for forgiveness and hearing or experiencing forgiveness with someone who can be a human mediator of God's forgiveness. This is why the idea of using the help of a spiritual director, pastoral counselor, or soul friend is significant. They can often be the agents God uses to bestow the healing grace of forgiveness. Even though I might be able to accept in my head the theological concept of God's forgiveness, I need to experience it in my heart and soul through another person. This is the key: being in relationship with someone who incarnates God's mercy, grace, and forgiveness."

The next time someone says, "You just have to forgive yourself," or when you know that you need help in accepting forgiveness, try an experiment. Get together with someone you trust and carefully apply Dr. Thiele's process of self-accepting-forgiveness:

1. You discuss your feelings of guilt.
2. You name whatever seems to be causing your guilt.
3. You express your personal remorse, regret, shame.
4. You genuinely and sincerely ask for God's help and forgiveness, especially as revealed in and through Jesus Christ.
5. You accept and receive the gift of forgiveness with a renewed spirit, a grateful heart, and a peace within that surpasses all understanding.

For a fuller explanation of "self-accepting forgiveness," you may contact Dr. William Thiele by email at Soulcare4u@aol.com.

Session 9

The Unforgivable Sin
And Self-Forgiveness

Study Guide

1. Begin with centering silence and prayer.

2. Ask someone to read Mark 3:28-29 aloud. This is a difficult passage to understand. These words of Jesus have prompted untold numbers of people to ask: "Am I guilty of having committed the unforgivable sin?" Has anyone in the group ever asked that question? Comments?

3. In "The Unforgivable Sin," notice the four subsections:

   • The context
   • Defining blasphemy
   • Related issues
   • Applying this teaching

   Divide the group into four, assigning one of the above subsections to each group. Have the smaller groups get together to review their assignments, discuss the material, and appoint someone to report the highlights of their conversations. After all four make their reports, invite discussion with the total group. (Note to the session leader: Decide how much time to use for the smaller groups and how much for the total group discussion.)
   At the conclusion of the group discussion, read Eugene H. Peterson's unique paraphrase of Mark 3:28-29.

4. Turn to "Self-Forgiveness." Three different understandings to this significant issue are presented. As your time permits, begin a discussion of self-forgiveness. Do not hurry through this material. What you do not cover in this session, continue in the next group meeting.

    Procedure: Have those who were assigned to make reports speak briefly on each of the three approaches to self-forgiveness, followed by group discussion.

5. Closure: Remind the group of the seminary professor's statement: "The only sin God cannot forgive is the sin that remains unconfessed." Close with silent moments of personal reflection and confession.

6. Homework: Study "Healing Related To Forgiveness Of Sin" in Session 10.

Session 10

Healing Related To Forgiveness Of Sin

When forgiveness occurs, an event of cosmic proportions takes place: divisions are healed and the world moves closer to the state in which it was created.
— Doris Donnelly

How significant is the forgiveness of sin in the healing process? Of the 25 recorded healing stories of Jesus in the four gospels, only two have direct references to forgiveness of sin. Both stories have some interesting similarities:

- The main characters with health problems are men.
- These men remain nameless to the readers.
- Both men are unable to walk.
- Neither man came to Jesus asking for help.
- Both are cured of their disabilities.

However, noticeable differences in the two stories cause us to explore the relationship between forgiveness of sin and healing.

The setting in John 5:1-15 is by the pool of Bethesda, where Jesus healed a man who had been paralyzed for 38 years. From the author's details, obviously this man had given up hope of ever walking again. Jesus took the initiative to speak with him. Notice that the first words of Jesus were not about helping him physically, but showed his concern for the man's mental attitude toward his despairing situation. "Do you want to be made well?" asked Jesus (John 15:6).

Rather than give Jesus a direct answer, the man began to make excuses about having no one to help him. Jesus ignored the man's response to his question and ordered him: "Stand up, take your mat and walk." At once the man was made well, and he took up his mat and began to walk (John 5:8-9). Later that same day, Jesus found the man in the temple and said to him, "See, you have been made well! Do not sin any more, so that nothing worse happens to you" (John 5:14). Does this mean that the now-cured, homeless man's paralysis had been caused by his sinfulness? We can only guess. Keep in mind that Jesus did not say to the man before he was healed, "Your sins are forgiven you." Forgiveness of the man's past sins is implied, but not spoken of directly in the healing process in this story.

The other healing story in Mark 2:1-12 (also recorded in Matthew 9:2-8 and Luke 5:17-26) reports that Jesus was at home in Capernaum. Not surprisingly, the house was too small to hold all who came to hear Jesus that day.

> *So many gathered around that there was no longer room*
> *for them not even in front of the door.*　　— Mark 2:2

Try to imagine the shock and amazement of everyone in the house, including Jesus, when, without permission or announcement, some people dug through the roof and lowered a paralyzed man lying on a stretcher. Deeply impressed by the faith and persistence of the sick man's friends, Jesus shifted from a teaching to a healing mode. Notice how different from the previous story are the first words spoken by Jesus to the paralytic:

> *Son, your sins are forgiven.*　　　　— Mark 2:5

Immediately this upset some of the religious leaders present in the room, who seriously questioned Jesus' authority to forgive sins, and who accused him of blasphemy. Jesus proceeded to engage these skeptics in a brief theological discussion. Then turning back to the man on the stretcher, Jesus completed the healing process.

"I say to you stand up, take your mat and go to your home." And he stood up, and immediately took the mat, and went out before all of them; so that they were all amazed and glorified God, saying, "We have never seen anything like this." — Mark 2:11-12

Tempting as it may be to unpack other issues raised in these two healing stories, our main focus is on the actions and words of Jesus dealing with sin, forgiveness, and health.

The word "sin" literally means missing the mark or falling short of the standards set by God for ethical and moral behavior, as well as for healthy bodies, minds, spirits, and relationships with others. In the Byzantine Liturgy, before receiving the Eucharist (Holy Communion), both priest and people pray together for the forgiveness of all sin, deliberate and indeliberate. In this context, sin is seen as anything that prevents God from being God in our life.[53]

Given the scriptural evidence that Jesus instinctively knew when forgiveness of sin was needed in certain unhealthy situations and not in others, what lessons can we learn from these stories? You may want to review the health benefits of forgiveness discussed in Session 3.

A primary question rising from these healing stories: Is all sickness caused by sin? Or, to make it more personal: Every time you get sick, does that mean you caused your illness by sinning? A connection between personal sin and personal sickness can exist, but not in all circumstances. Obviously, we bring on some of our own illnesses by making poor choices. It is estimated that 75 percent of all deaths in the United States before age 65 are premature, having been caused by personal, unhealthy lifestyle habits.[54]

Personal sickness and suffering can also be brought on by the consequences of other people's sins. The world today is a respecter of no one. Clearly, all illness is not due to personal sin; however, experience dictates and the Jesus way of forgiveness indicates that frequent examination of conscience, confession of sins, and receptivity to God's assurance of pardon are necessary to maintain a more healthy life.

Those who attend worship services that offer prayers for healing, primarily praying for release from pain and suffering of physical illnesses, may be overlooking a deeper need to experience forgiveness and healing of their relationships with God and other people. Refusing to acknowledge personal sin, or not seeking God's help in letting go of sin and guilt, can certainly be a barrier in the healing process. It is not accidental that confession of personal sin is incorporated in the healing instructions recorded by James.

> *Are any among you sick? They should call for the elders of the church and have them pray over them, anointing them with oil in the name of the Lord. The prayer of faith will save the sick, and the Lord will raise them up; and anyone who has committed sins will be forgiven. Therefore, confess your sins to one another, and pray for one another, so that you may be healed.*
> — James 5:14-16

The common saying, "Confession is good for the soul," could well be expanded.

> *"Confession is not only good for the soul, but equally beneficial to the body, the mind, and to one's many relationships in life." In Roman Catholic parishes throughout the world, the Sacrament of Reconciliation was implemented in 1975. Historically called the Sacrament of Penance or Confession, it is now renamed the Sacrament of Reconciliation because "it confers on the sinner the love of God who reconciles. 'Be reconciled to God' (2 Corinthians 5:20). Whoever lives in the merciful love of God will be prompt to respond to the invitation of the Lord: 'Go first and be reconciled with your brother' (Matthew 5:24)."*[55]

When Jesus helped the two men who suffered from physical paralysis, forgiveness of their personal sins was a critical factor in the healing process. Catholic, Orthodox, and Protestant traditions of the Christian faith continue to place a high value on confession and forgiveness in a holistic understanding of health.

Presbyterian Minister John Sutherland Bonnell offers an affirming observation:

> *We cannot fail to note that the confession and forgiveness of sins appear in some instances to have a determinative role in his healing miracles ... Whenever he said to those who came to him for healing, "Thy sins are forgiven thee, go in peace," we may be sure that the alienation from God within the life of the individual had first to be healed and his sins forgiven before he could receive the inner peace so sorely lacking.*[56]

John 5:1-15; Mark 2:1-12

Session 10

Healing Related To Forgiveness Of Sin

Study Guide
1. Begin with centering silence and prayer.

2. Discuss "Self-Forgiveness" from Session 9. Invite members of the group to share:

   • personal difficulties in practicing self-forgiveness and
   • ways that helped them in the process of self-forgiveness.

3. Turn to "Healing Related To Forgiveness Of Sin." Of the 25 healing stories of Jesus in the four gospels, only two have direct references to forgiveness of sin. Have each story read aloud in the group: John 5:1-15 and Mark 2:1-12.

4. Discuss comments, questions, and insights from the group related to these two stories.

5. Two questions surface from these stories:

   • Is all personal sickness caused by personal sin?
   • Are some personal illnesses not caused by personal sin?

   Invite the group to reflect on some specific times in their lives when they experienced personal illnesses. Did sin play a role or not? Discuss.

6. Closure: Read aloud the statement by John Sutherland Bonnell then ask the group to offer silent prayers of confession. Go with the assurance that God's unlimited forgiveness and redeeming grace continue to be freely given by Jesus Christ.

7. Homework: Study "Two Brothers And Their Father" in Session 11.

Session 11

Two Brothers And Their Father

To forgive is the highest, most beautiful form of love. In return, you will receive untold peace and happiness.
— Robert Muller

One of the best loved and often told human interest stories of Jesus is commonly titled, "The Parable Of The Prodigal Son." It's all about the Jesus way of forgiveness, yet the word "forgiveness" is not mentioned. Open your Bible and read Luke 15:11-32, slowly absorbing every detail. If you are already acquainted with this story, approach it with an open mind and heart, as if this is the very first reading. You may want to have a note pad and pen available to jot down questions, ideas, or insights arising from the text. Allow yourself to enter 100 percent into the story. Do not rush. Take your time.

Now read Luke 15:1-10, observing that chapter 15 of Luke contains three stories all related to the lost being found and the joyful celebrations that follow. Jesus addressed these parables of the "losts" to the Pharisees and the scribes who were grumbling and saying, "This fellow (Jesus) welcomes sinners and eats with them" (Luke 15:2). His audience that day could well have remained untouched by the stories of the lost sheep and the lost coin, but when Jesus boldly and deliberately added the third parable you can almost hear them murmuring, "Now he has stopped preaching and started meddling."

If Jesus had intended to focus only on the son who left home for a while, recklessly spending his inheritance, the story would have ended with verse 24. What about the other son, who dutifully stayed home obeying his father's every wish? His story is told in verses 25-32. Then there is the significant role of the father consistently caring about both sons throughout the story. More accurate titles for this dramatic narrative might be, "A Tale Of Two Prodigal Sons" or "The Story Of A Compassionate, Forgiving Father."

Taking a closer look at Luke 15:11-32, perhaps you are questioning the division of the inheritance before the death of the father. Under Jewish law of that period, in the case of two sons being in line to receive the family estate, the elder son must get two-thirds and the younger son one-third. (See Deuteronomy 21:17.) According to New Testament scholar William Barclay, "It was by no means unusual for a father to distribute his estate before he died if he wished to retire from the actual management of affairs."[57]

Why, we have to ask, is this parable ranked among the world's best short stories ever told? A logical answer is because the reader not only becomes quickly drawn into the unfolding plot, identifying with one or the other brother, but is also somewhat overwhelmed by the father's attitude and actions. From a human viewpoint, today's society would side with the elder son's response; however, the parables of Jesus are told from God's viewpoint. And because this particular parable powerfully communicates the unconditional love, limitless compassion, and abundant mercy of God, the reader silently wishes, hopes, and prays that God stands ready, even as the father in the story, to welcome home, to forgive, and to restore today's prodigal daughters and sons.

During the American Civil War, President Abraham Lincoln was asked how he was going to treat the rebellious southerners when they had finally been defeated and had returned to the Union of the United States. The questioner expected that vengeance would be Lincoln's post-war plan, but he answered, "I will treat them as if they had never been away." In this parable, this is exactly the way the father treats both sons, "as if they had never been away."[58]

Looking through the lens of forgiveness/unforgiveness, revisit Luke 15:11-32. The younger son is appropriately described as the prodigal, even though this word comes not from the lips of Jesus. "Prodigal" has a string of meanings ranging from "recklessly extravagant" to "outright wasteful." While we may note his lack of common sense, unwise decisions, and disrespect toward his father

116

by asking for his inheritance prematurely, when he at last "came to himself" and decided to return home, he was not expecting any favors, and least of all, forgiveness for his prodigality. He had to be more than surprised at his father's genuine joy and sincere welcome. He knew he deserved none of this, but God's grace, as displayed by the father, is never based on what we deserve, but rather on what God desires for us. We wonder how the younger son responded to all of this. Was he so overcome with his father's joyful reception that he re-entered the family circle, never to leave again? Or, did he take off after the party ended, having regained some of his losses?

The older son, as pictured by Jesus, is the opposite of everything embodied in the younger son. He is responsible, dependable, dutiful, and hardworking. Putting up with no nonsense, he set high standards for himself and others. He is totally legalistic, displaying an absence of mercy and forgiveness toward those who do not live up to his expectations, including his own family members. In a sense, the older brother is the prodigal who stayed home. Susan Ertz comments in her novel, *The Prodigal Heart*, "While the younger son was prodigal in body (and material wealth), at least part of his heart was always at home; but the elder brother was prodigal at heart, and only his body was at home."[59]

The older sibling had wasted many opportunities to share his wealth, which he received not because he deserved or earned it. He just happened to be the firstborn son. Likewise, he was blind to the lifelong love and blessings freely bestowed upon him by his father. All of this he spent lavishly on himself. He was the prodigal who stayed home.

Jesus portrays the older son as being totally upset and angry at his father and at his brother. He let the entire homecoming scene fill him with resentment and bitterness. Is he overreacting? Did he have the right to withhold forgiveness? What about all his years of faithfulness to his father? He is hurt, confused, and indignant! Did he have a change of heart or did he choose to remain outside the family celebrations? In today's family circles, the dutiful "older brothers" still persist in living a bittersweet relationship with their fathers. It doesn't have to be that way, but too often it is.

The father in Jesus' parable has typically been compared to God, our heavenly Father. The all-encompassing, unquestionable, no strings attached, kind of love demonstrated by the father for both of his sons has an unearthly, divine quality. The casual reader of Luke 15:11-32 can usually identify with one or the other brothers thinking, "Wow, that's me. Jesus really nailed my problem that may not be so obvious to other people."

However, could it be, is it possible, that Jesus was more interested in commending and elevating the role of the father than dwelling on the antics of the brothers? Is the thrust and focus of this parable on being and on becoming more and more like the father in the way we treat our family members, as well as those outside our immediate family? The heartbeat of this parable has common bloodlines with other so-called "radical" teachings of Jesus:

> *Be perfect as your heavenly Father is perfect.*
> — Matthew 5:48

> *Be merciful, just as your Father is merciful.*
> — Luke 6:36

In his book, *The Return of the Prodigal Son*, Henri Nouwen gets our attention with these insights:

> *If the only meaning of the story were that people sin but God forgives, I could easily begin to think of my sins as a fine occasion for God to show me forgiveness. There would be no real challenge in such an interpretation. I would resign myself to my weaknesses and keep hoping that eventually God would close (God's) eyes to them and let me come home, whatever I did. Such sentimental romanticism is not the message of the Gospels.*[60]

Nor is this the message of Jesus' parable of the two brothers and their father. Nouwen reminds us that we are children of God and joint heirs with Christ of blessings and riches beyond our imagining.

*Indeed, as son and heir I am to become successor. I am
destined to step into my Father's place and offer to others the same compassion that (God) has offered me.
The return to the Father is ultimately the challenge to
become the Father.*[61]

And how does one go about becoming more and more like our
spiritual Father? By adopting the Jesus forgiveness model as our
personal lifelong practice and by constantly seeking divine assistance and encouragement, we can begin to make some progress
toward this worthy goal. Nouwen shares his personal experiences
in trying to become more like the Father.

*It is this divine forgiveness that I have to practice in my
daily life. It calls me to keep stepping over all my argu-
ments that say forgiveness is unwise, unhealthy, and
impractical. It challenges me to step over all my needs
for gratitude and compliments. Finally, it demands of
me that I step over that wounded part of my heart that
feels hurt and wronged and that wants to stay in control and put a few conditions between me and the one
whom I am asked to forgive.*[62]

The Jesus way of forgiveness, as illustrated in this parable,
teaches us, male and female alike, to acknowledge the younger
and older brother within each of us and to release it all to our understanding, merciful God. It is in repeatedly receiving God's gift
of forgiveness that we are empowered and motivated to give to
others the gift of forgiveness.

As Leonard J. Biallas comments in his book, *World Religions*,
Christianity is

*... a gift that can be accepted or rejected. It is a reli-
gion established on the word of forgiveness and the
healing touch of Jesus ... It is so hard for us to accept
that God is compassionate, like the prodigal's father,
and loves us inspite of ourselves ... in forgiveness there
is a sense of giftedness. Persons can choose death by*

not forgiving; they can destroy themselves by not say-
ing "yes" to justice, to celebration. Forgiveness is the
great "yes" to life.[63]

Session II

Two Brothers And Their Father

Study Guide

1. Begin with centering silence and prayer.

2. Open your Bibles to Luke 15:11-32. Assign parts to the group members. You will need the following characters to speak their lines in this dramatic reading.

_____ Jesus or narrator
_____ Younger son
_____ Father
_____ Older son
_____ Servant

3. After reading this story, invite initial reactions from the group.

4. Typical reader response to this timeless parable of Jesus has been to identify in a personal way with one of the two brothers; however, could it be that Jesus was more interested in commending and elevating the role of the father then dwelling on the antics of the sons? Is the dominate focus of this narrative on being and on becoming more and more like the father in the way we treat our family members, as well as those outside our immediate family? Discuss.

5. Resent, resentment, and resentful are words that describe harmful, negative feelings. One of the root meanings of "resent" is to resend or to relive personal hurts and insults, to hold on to persistent ill will toward another person. The older brother

harbored his resentment toward his father and younger brother for years, but then it spewed out toward the end of the parable. Unlike outright anger and revenge, resentment is subtle, sneaks up on us, but stays hidden much of the time. Discuss.

6. This is sometimes called an open-ended parable of Jesus. Why did Jesus not wrap it up by telling us what happened next? Perhaps he intended his listeners (and Luke intended for his readers) to draw their own conclusions. Letting your imagination be your guide, try writing three different endings.

    The first ending is fairly easy to do. Focusing on the three principal characters, the two brothers and their father, what do you think may have happened next? Describe their ongoing relationships.

    The second ending is somewhat harder. Put yourself in the sandals of the first hearers of this parable, the Pharisees and the religious scholars. What impact would this trilogy of "lost and found" stories in Luke 15 have had on them? Imagine their talk-back and responses to Jesus.

    The third ending is more difficult, but not impossible. In your family circles, are there strained, fractured, or unhealthy relationships? Do you feel a personal kinship with the father or either of the two brothers? If so, what would be the shape of your ending script, as you allow this parable to connect with you and your family situations?

    If time permits, take ten minutes for the group members to reflect and write. Then invite discussion with some volunteering to read their creative endings.

7. Closure: Offer prayer, silently and spoken, for the compassionate, seeking love of God to help relationships that need healing.

8. Homework: Study "The Supreme Example Of Forgiveness" in Session 12.

Session 12

The Supreme Example
Of Forgiveness

Forgiveness is not a natural response without some grace-filled intervention. — Ronald E. Swisher

While enduring incredible, horrific suffering, as he hung from his cross, Jesus uttered some of his most profound words. According to Luke's gospel the very first sentence coming from the lips of Jesus at the time of his crucifixion is this:

> *"Father, forgive them; for they do not know what they are doing."* — Luke 23:34

Here is the supreme example of forgiveness. Although it defies logical explanation, at the same time it draws us into the very heart and spirit of Jesus. Given the circumstances that led to his death, how could Jesus have been so forgiving? To whom is Jesus referring in his prayer by "them" and "they"? Is he wanting to forgive certain leaders of the religious establishment who had plotted for years to eliminate him? Is he forgiving the Roman soldiers who were dutifully carrying out their orders? Is he forgiving his close circle of disciples, who all but abandoned him in his final hours?

We note, also, that Jesus' petitionary prayer to his heavenly Father is based on "them" not knowing "what they are doing." Is Jesus implying that they lack understanding of him and his mission or that they are pawns in a larger drama beyond their control? Exactly what did Jesus mean? These questions, while raising one's curiosity, must not detract from our main focus: the consistency of Jesus in teaching and modeling forgiveness throughout his public ministry and until his last breath.

123

We have taken a close look at several forgiveness episodes in the life of Jesus. These form the scriptural basis for "The Jesus Paradigm." We could safely say that Jesus' noble and generous prayer of forgiveness from the cross is a culmination of a lifetime of constantly forgiving whenever forgiveness is needed. We could convincingly say that what Jesus taught in the Sermon on the Mount about loving one's enemies, blessing those who persecute you, and praying for those who harm you, he demonstrated painfully and genuinely.

The word that may best describe Jesus' way of forgiveness is "initiator." Taking the initiative in activating the forgiveness process characterized his entire ministry. Flora Wuellner is quite correct in saying that throughout his life, Jesus had a great deal to forgive.

> *People in his hometown, Nazareth, tried to execute him; his own mother and brothers at one point (thinking he was deranged) tried to have him restrained; the authorities continually set traps for him and tried to lead him into self-recrimination; his own disciples sometimes tried to block his path; many towns refused to welcome him; Judas betrayed him; Peter denied him; most of his disciples fled from the scene after his arrest.*[64]

The easiest path would have been to give up and give in, but not God's specially begotten son, God's anointed one whom we have come to know as reconciler, healer, counselor, savior, and forgiver. Jesus, the initiator, freely offered God's grace and mercy to everyone. The authors of the book, *The Rivers of Paradise*, remind us of this uniqueness in Christianity.

> *The promise of salvation to sinners is the undeniably distinctive characteristic of Jesus' message. The forgiveness that Jesus announced did not require the offering of the Temple sacrifices that were the prescribed means of atoning for sin. Jesus proclaimed God's love to "sinners" before they repented.*[65]

124

The person expressing forgiveness on the cross is the same Jesus whose forgiveness was his lifestyle.

> *More deeply than mere words, he forgave, even when forgiveness was not asked. On the night in which he was betrayed he broke and shared the bread with all his disciples, knowing that one would betray him, another deny him, and that all would flee from him ... later on the shores of Lake Tiberias he lovingly healed Peter of his deep shame. Understanding, compassion, release, and healing flowed from Jesus' heart to all who hurt him.*[66]

Jesus' supreme act of forgiveness on the cross made a lasting impact on early Christians, many of whom put their lives on the line for their faith and beliefs. Stephen, the first Christian martyr, courageously followed Jesus' example. Given the sentence of death by stoning, he prayed, "Lord, Jesus, receive my spirit." Then he knelt down and cried out in a loud voice, "Lord, do not hold this sin against them" (Acts 7:59-60).

Furthermore, the Jesus way of forgiveness continues to motivate and influence countless numbers of Christians, who offer forgiveness in extreme situations that stretch human endurance to the breaking point. Coming out of World War II is the amazing forgiveness story from the heart and pen of Corrie ten Boom, who along with her beloved sister, Betsie, were placed in a German concentration camp for their participation in the Dutch underground movement. Betsie's death at the hands of her captors had a lifelong impact on Corrie. After the war ended in 1945, Corrie became a good-will ambassador for Jesus, doing her best to bring the gospel of forgiveness and healing to many, many people. She traveled throughout her native Holland, as well as other parts of Europe and the United States. But the place where the (spiritual) hunger seemed greatest was Germany.

One evening after speaking in a church service, she recognized a former Nazi guard who made a point to thank her for her gospel message of forgiveness. That was a defining moment for Corrie as she prayed silently for Jesus' help in forgiving this man. She could not do it on her own. In her words:

> *As I took his hand the most incredible thing happened. From my shoulder along my arm and through my hand a current seemed to pass from me to him, while in my heart sprang a love for this stranger that almost overwhelmed me. And so I discovered that it is not on our forgiveness any more than on our goodness that the world's healing hinges, but on His. When He (Jesus) tells us to love our enemies, He gives, along with the command, the love itself.*[67]

Then there is Terry Anderson, the American journalist who was held captive by terrorists in Lebanon for 2,545 days in the 1980s. During the years since his release he has shared his faith and forgiveness with many audiences. "When I speak about forgiveness," he said, "I am speaking totally about my personal experiences, my own feelings and my own search. I cannot speak for anyone else. It's hard to get past the words that are right there on the very first page of our contract with God. That's the place where it says, 'Forgive us our trespasses, as we forgive those who trespass against us.' " Anderson said his wife once described the lessons they have learned this way: "If you want the joy, you can't have the anger." Consider his thoughts about the attacks on the New York World Trade Center on September 11, 2001.

> *The people that kidnapped me, just like the people who committed this terrible atrocity, are not sorry today. They are not asking for forgiveness. No, forgiveness is about what is in me. Hatred and anger are terribly debilitating. They are soul-destroying. We have every reason to be angry at those people ... but anger will lead us into places where we do not want to go.*[68]

Is it easy to forgive the one who harms you or someone you love? No. Is it easy to forgive someone who slanders our reputation or shatters our dreams? No. Is it easy to extend forgiveness to the one who uses us for personal gain? No. But it is possible.

126

In my earlier book, *Blessed to Be a Blessing*, I shared my personal convictions about the supreme act of forgiveness. By his personal example Jesus demonstrated what it means to forgive whenever forgiveness is called for, whether or not we feel like forgiving. When he was dying on the cross, he did not wait until his enemies apologized. He did not wait until he was feeling good before he prayed, "Father, forgive them; for they know not what they do." If anyone had the right to be unforgiving, it was the innocent, crucified Jesus who died expressing forgiveness.[69]

The next time anyone hurts or harms you in any way, remember that an unforgiving attitude is incompatible with the forgiving heart and spirit of Jesus Christ. Because of our humanness we may be upset, angry, disturbed, and unforgiving — temporarily. However, when we take the name Christian and are committed to living a Christlike life, we forfeit all rights and privileges to withhold forgiveness permanently. Flora Wuellner rightly concludes, "Forgiveness is a person. Forgiveness has a face."[70]

That person and that face is Jesus.

The Anatomy Of Forgiveness

Author's Note: This essay comes from the heart, spirit, and life-experiences of Danny E. Morris, United Methodist minister, prolific author, popular speaker, and inspiring retreat leader. Danny had a creative hand in initiating and developing the Academy for Spiritual Formation, the Emmaus Walk, the Upper Room Prayer Ministry, the Discernment Network, a journal of the Christian spiritual life called "Weavings," the John Wesley Great Experiment, and the Ecumenical Monastic Community. Here Danny shares what he has learned and is learning about God's amazing gift of forgiveness, especially when forgiveness seems to be impossible.

The woman was devastated that her husband had been unfaithful in their marriage eleven years earlier. When he died, she had not been able to (or had not wanted to) forgive him. Because she has not, and felt she cannot forgive, she is hooked on hurt and hate.

These negative attitudes have taken over her life and she is an emotional cripple. She said she can't relate in loving ways to her children nor even to her grandchildren.

Many people have told her that she must forgive her husband or she will never be free from him. She agrees. She has tried to, but she has been unable to forgive. A painful hurt has been hooked into her spirit for more than eleven years. A visible result of her inability to forgive is the deep scowl that has been etched into her face. Her countenance is so empty and forlorn, one wonders how long it has been since she laughed. If it had been possible, she would have dealt with his betrayal at the time it happened, but how to do that? During the intervening years she has found no way to forgive, and when he died outside of her forgiveness, it was like another nail had been driven into the coffin of her unforgiveness. Everything about her story, her sense of being broken, and her appearance cry out, "What can I do?"

Several unhelpful answers, without any practical guidelines, have been offered in response to her devastating question.

- Forgive your husband.
- Forgive him for what he did.
- Forgive him for hurting you so deeply.
- Forgive him for enslaving you to his hurtful wrong.

All of these are what I call "non-stick answers." She continues to anguish and weep over her version of a question that many people have asked, "How do I forgive when I can't?" I have no soft, or easy, or final answer, only shared experiences and some discoveries along the way. Her question prompts a hard saying, "You have to forgive!" Let me say it another way, "You must forgive!" To forgive is hard and often painful, but not to forgive has unwanted negative consequences.

- Not to forgive means that one is forever bound to the person or the deed.
- Not to forgive creates a permanent enslavement to the heinous memory.

- Not to forgive drains and restrains the rest of one's life.
- Not to forgive is an option, but not a positive solution.

Let me illustrate with my memory of an actual forgiveness episode from the early days of our marriage. Rosalie and I stood on the brink of non-forgiveness. Nothing had produced in us a greater sense of panic. Since I am not there now, I can see some things that helped when I was there.

First, I realized that intentional forgiveness is possible. Many people have forgiven worse things than I have faced.

Second, I discovered that forgiveness is a science. Certain conditions are necessary in the process of forgiveness because they are causal. For example, one begins with an intention to forgive. Although the intention to forgive may be tentative and non-active, it is the place to begin, because it causes something else to happen. A growing intention to forgive creates a desire to forgive. Unless forgiveness becomes a desire of one's heart, forget it — which is exactly what you will do! A desire is far more powerful than an intention. If I have a desire to forgive, it is solidly anchored within me.

Desire is also causal because it enables action, and action is an essential part of forgiveness. Forgiveness is never passive nor docile and it does not just happen when we are not looking. Forgiveness does not drop out of the blue into our laps. Forgiveness happens as a direct result of something we do. Our forgiveness of another requires that we are totally involved in the process.

Third, I discovered that there is also an art to forgiveness. When Rosalie and I were first married, we experienced a deep hurt from a close friend. He defiled our friendship by willfully spreading the rumor within the congregation I served that our first child was conceived out of wedlock. We laughed when we first heard the rumor because we knew that was simply not possible. However, he persisted with the rumor and the result became ugly and hurtful. Ten months later, our first son was born.

As I reflected on that experience, it was like we stood before an empty canvas and we could choose what to put there — our broken spirits, despair, hate, unceasing anguish — or what? Instead of these colors, we chose to take it in stages ... like an artist applies paint. Rather than be eaten up with hate and its resulting hurt, we chose to forgive. This was all we knew to do at the time. We thought it best to forgive him and move on with our lives. For several weeks our intention to forgive was our only place to stand, so we began to try to do it.

Eventually, after several months, we could say, "We have forgiven him." We severed our relationship with him, not because we hated or even disliked him. But, we had learned to stay away from him, just as one learns to give space to a very hot stove. This happened many years ago. Because we made the right choice of what to put on our canvas we have had some forty years of freedom from a terrible and hurtful betrayal of a one-time close friendship.

We used four colors from our artist's palate. At various stages of our experience of forgiveness we could say:

1. We want to forgive (intention leads to desire).
2. We are forgiving (make a conscious decision to forgive).
3. We have forgiven (time and healed memory are revealing).
4. We have freedom from hurt (in bondage no more).

We learned that there is an art to forgiveness and that forgiveness is a beautiful picture that is worth painting.

Fourth, we said forgiveness is a science, as well as an art; but ultimately, forgiveness is a gift from God that provides a person with the power to forgive. This is the heart and the heartbeat of the anatomy of forgiveness. There are attitudes to hold, steps to take, conditions to meet, and accomplishments to attain, but all of these are only preparatory to receiving the gift of the power to forgive, which God is eager to give to the brokenhearted. How to forgive "when we can't forgive" is through the gift of a spiritual power beyond human capacities. Forgiveness power is an ultimate form of spiritual power. It is a power to be prayed for, as in "... forgive us our sins, as we forgive those who sin against us ..." (Matthew 6:12). Receive this eternal, trustworthy truth: God, whom we have come to know as Father, Son, and Holy Spirit, along with all the company of heaven and all of the loving, caring people who surround you, wants you to receive the gift of the power to forgive.

We all wish that forgiveness could happen swiftly, but it usually requires time. We must devote all of the time necessary to developing a forgiving spirit and to continuing to pray for the spiritual gift that will empower forgiveness. A forgiving spirit is a definite upgrade over a hateful or vengeful spirit. A forgiving spirit will enable you to receive and give the gift of forgiveness. It may be that the gift enabling you to forgive is God's favorite gift to give you![71]

The Supreme Example Of Forgiveness

Study Guide

1. Begin with centering silence and prayer.

2. Turn to the author's commentary on Luke 23:34 in "The Supreme Example Of Forgiveness." Discuss questions, reflections, and observations.

3. These words of Jesus from his cross are only recorded in Luke's gospel. Have someone read aloud the context of this sentence, what went before and after. See Luke 23:32-43. Discuss the thoughts, feelings, and emotions of Jesus. Why do you think Jesus took the initiative in requesting forgiveness from his heavenly Father?

4. Try to recall your most memorable experience:

   • in not being forgiven when you wanted to be forgiven.
   • in being forgiven and knowing personal forgiveness.

   After reflecting on these two personal experiences, invite members to voluntarily share their responses with the group.

5. The next time anyone hurts or harms you in anyway, intentionally remember that an unforgiving attitude is incompatible with the forgiving heart and spirit of Jesus. Because of our humanness we may be upset, angry, disturbed, and unforgiving — temporarily. However, when we take the name Christian and

are committed to living as a Christian, we forfeit all rights and privileges to withhold forgiveness permanently.

- If there is someone you need to forgive in your life, do not put it off. Just do it and let that person know you have forgiven. Initiate the forgiveness process.
- If there is someone from whom you need to ask forgiveness in your life, do not put it off. Just do it. Be a forgiveness initiator (like Jesus).

6. Closure: This is your last group session. Take a few moments to share what this study of the Jesus way of forgiveness has meant to the group members. What are some learnings, insights, continuing struggles, and positive forgiveness experiences?

It would be most appropriate to conclude with Holy Communion. Invite your pastor or another clergyperson to preside at the Lord's table. Then go in peace, knowing that the peace of the forgiving, merciful, compassionate Christ goes with you always.

A Guided Group Prayer
Of Forgiveness

Preparation: Invite the group to enter into this guided prayer, remembering that forgiveness is a process not an event. Prepare for an uninterrupted, unhurried time of prayer. Get as comfortable as possible, breathing deeply, relaxing your mind and body, being open and receptive to the Holy Spirit. Someone will then pray the following prayer aloud.

We adore you, O Christ, we praise you, O Christ, because through your holy cross you have redeemed the world and saved each of us from our sins.

Through your holy cross you have forgiven us and loved us even before we knew what forgiveness and love were all about. *(pause)*

Right now, O Christ, each one of us comes to you seeking help in being a forgiving person. *(pause)*

Some of us are having difficulty forgiving. We need your strength and a willingness to be willing to forgive. Help each of us overcome stubbornness and pride that cripple us in so many ways. *(pause)*

And now, O Christ, in a conscious, deliberate act of our will, we want to forgive everyone who has anything against any of us.

Some of us need to forgive our parents. *(pause)*

Some of us need to forgive our children. *(pause)*

Some of us need to forgive God. *(pause)*

Some of us need to forgive ourselves. *(pause)*

Some of us need to forgive someone who died. *(pause)*

O Christ, receive our prayers as we pray by name for specific persons. *(pause for personal prayers of forgiveness in silence ... do not rush)*

And now, O Christ, we turn over to you ourselves and all those persons we have named in this prayer of forgiveness. As you direct any of us to take tangible action, give us the will to follow through (perhaps a phone call, an email message, a personal letter, an apology, or restitution).

Gracious and merciful Christ, help each one of us to know the joy of forgiveness; the joy of burdens taken away; the joy of new beginnings; the joy of health and wholeness in body, mind, spirit, and in all relationships. In the name of the Father, the Son, and the Holy Spirit, we pray and dedicate ourselves. Amen.[72]

Afterword

"Yes ... But"

Dear Reader:

I want to share a personal word with you. Because forgiveness is more grace and mercy than it is rules and regulations, this book has been quite challenging to research and write. I do not assume or pretend to have covered all of your personal issues and questions about forgiveness. Every time I speak on this topic, whether from the pulpit or in a workshop setting, someone always responds, politely and firmly:

"Yes, what you have presented sounds good, 'but' ...."
"Yes, I have read and heard much on this subject, 'but' ...."
"Yes, granted forgiveness is helpful in some situations, 'but' ...."
"Yes, I offered an apology, 'but' ...."
"Yes, Jesus certainly taught and lived forgiveness, 'but' ...."

My guess would be that all of those who are seriously looking for help with unforgiveness, resentfulness, bitterness, anger, abuse, and injustice could come up with more than a few "Yes ... but" scenarios. Human experience is an unrelenting, harsh schoolmaster. Life's lessons learned the hard way leave little space or desire to develop a forgiving heart and a merciful attitude. Some have even decided that certain categories of destructive, violent, bad behavior are outside the realm of forgiveness. From a human viewpoint, the "Yes ... but" exceptions to giving and receiving forgiveness seem limitless. But then, along came this one they call Jesus of Nazareth who also had some "Yes ... buts" to offer on the significance of forgiveness.

> *[YES] You have heard that it was said, "An eye for and eye and a tooth for a tooth." BUT I say to you, do not resist an evildoer. BUT if anyone strikes you on the right cheek, turn the other also.* — Matthew 5:38-39

[YES] You have heard that it was said, "You shall love your neighbor and hate your enemies." BUT I say to you, Love your enemies and pray for those who persecute you. — Matthew 5:43-44

To the woman caught in adultery, Jesus said,

[YES, I know you have been accused, BUT] I do not condemn you. Go your way, and from now on do not sin again. — John 8:10-11

Then Peter came and said to Jesus,

"Lord, if another member of the church sins against me, how often should I forgive? As many as seven times?" Jesus said to him, "[YES, I know some teach that.] I say to you, not seven times, BUT, I tell you, seventy times seven." — Matthew 18:21-22

As Jesus hung on the cross suffering unbearable pain, he could well have thought, "YES, I have every right to die with hatred in my heart toward those who are crucifying me." BUT instead, Jesus breathed aloud:

"Father, forgive them; for they do not know what they are doing." — Luke 23:34

To paraphrase the teachings and thoughts of Jesus: "*Yes*, I understand your situation, *but* there is another option. There are ways to break out of your unhealthy, unforgiving, bitter attitude. There are alternatives in getting unstuck from your painful past. Before you give up completely, try my way of forgiveness."

To harbor and withhold unforgiveness (whatever the circumstance) is to invite spiritual suicide and a giant dose *of* unhealthiness, physically and mentally. To work (and it is work) at developing a lifestyle of giving and receiving forgiveness is the Jesus way to personal wholeness, healthiness, and a new sense of freedom, as you experience release, relief, and renewal.

I wish it were possible to sit down with you, face to face, and talk about your "Yes ... buts." I would welcome sharing your personal situation and looking with you at some possibilities in moving on with your life.

I encourage you, not only to practice the guidelines to forgiveness as outlined in this book, but also to make an appointment with a minister, a pastor, a priest, a counselor, or a spiritual director, sharing honestly your "Yes ... buts" with a willingness to be willing to pursue the Jesus way.

I congratulate you for opening this book. Whether you merely surfed the contents or dug into some of the facts and facets or devoured every word, you have taken a positive step. You are expressing your frustration as well as your fascination, your resistance, as well as your resolve to giving and receiving forgiveness this day and in all your days ahead. Something may be prompting, encouraging, or directing you to breakout of your self-imposed, unforgiving attitudes and actions. That something could well be God calling you to try to live the Jesus way of forgiveness.

A Prayer For Coping With The "Yes ... Buts" Of Life

Forgiving and merciful God, I want to be honest with you right now. I know I am helpless without your help in being a forgiving person every time forgiveness is called for. Even though I am so very grateful for your blessings of compassion and pardon for me whenever I mess up my life, there are times when I find it totally impossible to forgive people who mess up my life and my loved ones. This is one of those times.

Today I am dealing with a particular, personal situation. *(describe the details, taking as much time as you need)* Yes, I know in my head I need to forgive and move on, *but* in my heart I am hurting and without your help I'm stuck. I guess I'm tired of living with the negative consequences of my arrogant attitude, damaged emotions, and precious pride.

I'm unsure what needs to be done next or if I'm even willing to try. Therefore, only your grace, your wisdom, your love, and the empowering presence of your Holy Spirit can make forgiveness possible in my heart, in my head, in my actions, in my words, and in my life.

Thank you, God, for listening to my plight and my plea. Now I will quiet myself and simply listen to you. *(take your time, do not rush)* As I continue seeking your help, give me the courage to let go and let the Jesus way of forgiveness be my way. In the name of Jesus I offer this prayer. Amen.

Recommended Resources

Barclay, William. *The Lord's Prayer*. Louisville: Westminster John Knox Press, 2001.

Countryman, L. William. *Forgiven and Forgiving*. Harrisburg, Pennsylvania: Morehouse Publishing, 1998.

Donnelly, Doris. *Learning To Forgive*. Nashville: Abingdon Press, 1979.

Donnelly, Doris. *Putting Forgiveness Into Practice*. Allen, Texas: Argus Communications, 1982.

Dyja, Thomas. *Forgiving and Being Forgiven*. New York: Marlowe & Company, 2001.

Jampolsky, Gerald G. *Forgiveness: The Greatest Healer of All*. Hillsboro, Oregon: Beyond Words Publishing, Inc., 1999.

Jones, Robert D. *Forgiveness: I Just Can't Forgive Myself*. Phillipsburg, New Jersey: P&R Publishing Company, 2000.

Ko-I Bastis, Madeline. *Heart of Forgiveness*. Boston: Red Wheel/Weiser, LLC, 2003.

Kushner, Harold S. *How Good Do We Have To Be?* New York: Little, Brown & Company, 1996.

Luskin, Fred. *Forgive For Good*. New York: Harper-Collins Publishing, 2002.

Maloney, George A. *Your Sins Are Forgiven You*. Staten Island: Alba House, 1994.

McCullough, Michael E., Pargament, Kenneth I., Thoresen, Carl E. *Forgiveness: Theory, Research, and Practice.* New York: The Guilford Press, 2000.

Meninger, William A. *The Process of Forgiveness.* New York: Continuum Publishing Company, 2001.

Nouwen, Henri J. M. *The Return of The Prodigal Son.* New York: Doubleday, 1992.

Rutledge, Thom. *The Self-Forgiveness Handbook.* Oakland, California: New Harbinger Publishing, 1997.

Smedes, Lewis B. *Forgive and Forget.* New York: Harper & Row, Publishing, 1984.

Smedes, Lewis B. *The Art of Forgiving.* Nashville: Moorings, a Division of Random House, Inc., 1996.

Stokes, Gillian. *Forgiveness: Wisdom From Around the World.* Boston: Red Wheel/Weiser, LLC, 2002.

Thompson, Marjorie J. *Soul Feast: An Invitation to the Christian Spiritual Life.* Louisville, Kentucky: Westminster John Knox Press, 1995.

Steere, Douglas *The Way of Forgiveness* (Nashville: Upper Room Books, 2002), participant's book in the series "Companions in Christ," p. 65.

Wagner, James K. *An Adventure in Healing and Wholeness.* Nashville: Upper Room Books, 1993.

Wagner, James K. *The Spiritual Heart of Your Health.* Nashville: Upper Room Books, 2002.

Weaver, Andrew J. and Furlong, Monica. *Reflections on Forgiveness and Spiritual Growth.* Nashville: Abingdon Press, 2000.

Wuellner, Flora S. *Release.* Nashville: Upper Room Books, 1996.

Wuellner, Flora S. *Forgiveness, the Passionate Journey.* Nashville: Upper Room Books, 2001.

Internet Web Sites

A Campaign For Forgiveness Research
Contact Robert Coles, M.D.
www.forgiving.org
Telephone 804-828-1193

ForgivenessNet
Contact Andrew Knock
www.forgivenessnet.co.uk
email: andrew@forgivenessnet.co.uk

Sources Of Epigraphs
In Section Headings

Page 4 [not numbered]: Robert D. Enright and Joanna North, editors, *Exploring Forgiveness* (Madison, Wisconsin: University of Wisconsin Press, 1998), Archbishop Desmond Tutu quote in the Foreword, p. xiii.

Page 19: Gillian Stokes, *Forgiveness* (York Beach, Maine: Red Wheel/ Weiser Publishers, 2002), Dag Hammarskjold quote, p. 62.

Page 31: Gillian Stokes, *Forgiveness* (York Beach, Maine: Red Wheel/ Weiser Publishers, 2002), *The New Oxford English Dictionary*, 1998, quote, p. 7.

Page 41: G. Ernest Thomas, *Adventurous Living* (Dayton, Ohio: U. T. S. Press, 1998), p. 136.

Page 49: Fred Luskin, *Forgive For Good* (New York: Harper Collins Publishers, 2002), Lord Herbert quote, p. 154.

Page 57: Saint Francis of Assisi, in *Putting Forgiveness Into Practice*, by Doris Donnelly (Allen, Texas: Argus Communications, 1982), p. 32.

Page 66: Robert D. Enright and Joanna North, editors, *Exploring Forgiveness* (Madison, Wisconsin: University of Wisconsin Press, 1998), Archbishop Desmond Tutu quote in the Foreword, p. xiii.

Page 71: Harold S. Kushner, *How Good Do We Have To Be?* (Boston, Massachusetts: Little, Brown and Company, 1996), p. 111.

Page 79: Rueben P. Job and Norman Shawchuck, *A Guide To Prayer For All God's People* (Nashville: Upper Room Books, 1990), Paula Ripple quote, p. 361.

Page 87: Flora S. Wuellner, *Forgiveness, The Passionate Journey* (Nashville: Upper Room Books, 2001), p. 35.

Page 95: Gillian Stokes, *Forgiveness* (York Beach, Maine: Red Wheel/ Weiser Publishers, 2002), anonymous quote, p. 125.

Page 107: Doris Donnelly, *Learning To Forgive* (Nashville: Abingdon Press, 1979), p. 99.

Page 115: Gillian Stokes, *Forgiveness* (York Beach, Maine: Red Wheel/ Weiser Publishers, 2002), Robert Muller quote, p. 64.

Page 123: Ronald E. Swisher, in *Reflections on Forgiveness and Spiritual Growth*, edited by Andrew J. Weaver and Monica Furlong (Nashville: Abingdon Press, 2000), p. 134.

Endnotes

1. James K. Wagner, *The Spiritual Heart of Your Health* (Nashville: Upper Room Books, 2002), pp. 23-24.

2. Alexander Pope, quoted by Garret Keizer in his article, "The Other Side of Rage," in *The Christian Century* magazine (Chicago: Christian Century Foundation Publishing. Vol. 119, No. 6, July 31-August 13, 2002), p. 23.

3. *Ibid*, p. 23.

4. Robert D. Enright and Joanna North, editors, *Exploring Forgiveness* (Madison, Wisconsin: The University of Wisconsin Press, 1998), Archbishop Desmond Tutu in the Foreword, p. xiii.

5. L. William Countryman, *Forgiven and Forgiving* (Harrisburg, Pennsylvania: Morehouse Publishing, 1998), p. 75.

6. Douglas Steere, *The Way of Forgiveness* (Nashville: Upper Room Books, 2002), participant's book in the series "Companions in Christ," p. 65.

7. Robert Schuller, *Life's Not Fair, But God Is Good* (Nashville: Thomas Nelson, Inc., 1991).

8. James Ross, "Forgiveness" an educational pamphlet published by the International Order of St. Luke The Physician, San Antonio, Texas, June/July 2002.

9. *Strong's Exhaustive Concordance of the Bible* (Nashville: Abingdon Press, 1980), pp. 486-487.

10. Marjorie J. Thompson, article "Moving Toward Forgiveness," *Weavings* magazine (Nashville: The Upper Room, Vol. VII, No. 2, 1992), p. 19.

11. Marjorie J. Thompson, *The Way of Forgiveness* (Nashville: Upper Room Books, 2002), p. 61.

12. Flora S. Wuellner, *Forgiveness, The Passionate Journey* (Nashville: Upper Room Books, 2001), p. 21.

13. John S. Mogabgab, Editor's Introduction in *Weavings* magazine (Nashville: The Upper Room, Vol. VII, No. 2, 1992), p. 2.

14. Lewis B. Smedes, *Forgive and Forget* (San Francisco: Harper & Row, 1984), pp. xi-xii.

15. Henri J. M. Nouwen, article "Forgiveness: the Name of Love in a Wounded World," *Weavings* magazine (Nashville: The Upper Room, Vol. VII, No. 2, 1992), p. 15.

16. Doris Donnelly, *Putting Forgiveness Into Practice* (Allen, Texas: Argus Communications, 1982), p. ix.

17. Doris Donnelly, *Learning to Forgive* (Nashville: Abingdon Press, 1979), p. 61.

18. Harry Camp's "Steps in Forgiveness" in a letter to James K. Wagner, November 2003.

19. Fred Luskin, *Forgive For Good* (New York: Harper Collins Publishing, 2002), p. xv.

20. *Ibid*, p. 80.

21. *Ibid*, p. 80.

22. *Ibid*, p. xv.

23. James K. Wagner, *Blessed To Be A Blessing* (Nashville: Upper Room Books, 1980), pp. 78-79.

24. Dale A. Matthews, *The Faith Factor* (New York: Viking-Penquin, 1998), p. 46.

25. James K. Wagner, *An Adventure in Healing and Wholeness* (Nashville: Upper Room Books, 1993), p. 42.

26. *Op cit*, Marjorie J. Thompson, article "Moving Toward Forgiveness," p. 21.

27. *Op cit*, Marjorie J. Thompson, *The Way of Forgiveness*, p. 82.

28. *Ibid*, pp. 87-88.

29. *Op cit*, James K. Wagner, *An Adventure in Healing and Wholeness*, pp. 53-54.

30. William Barclay, *The Lord's Prayer* (Louisville: Westminster John Knox Press, 2001), p. 50.

31. *Op cit, Strong's Exhaustive Concordance*, section on the Greek Dictionary of the New Testament, pp. 71 and 73.

32. William Barclay, *The Gospel of Matthew*, Vol. 1, The Daily Bible Study Series, Revised Edition (Philadelphia: Westminster Press, 1975), p. 222.

33. *Ibid*, p. 222.

34. *Ibid*, pp. 222-223.

35. *Ibid*, p. 178.

36. Maxie Dunnam and Kimberly Dunnam Reisman, *The Workbook on Virtues and Fruit of the Spirit* (Nashville: Upper Room Books, 1998), p. 136.

37. Charles L. Allen, *God's Seven Wonders For You* (Old Tappen, New Jersey: Fleming H. Revell Company, 1987), p. 67.

38. Michael E. McCullough, Kenneth I. Pargament, Carl E. Thorsesen, editors, *Forgiveness: Theory, Research, and Practice* (New York: The Guilford Press, 2000), "Religious Perspectives on Forgiveness," pp. 37-39.

39. William Barclay, *The Gospel of Matthew*, Vol. 2, The Daily Bible Study Series, Revised Edition (Philadelphia: Westminster Press, 1975), p. 193.

40. Halford E. Luccock, *Studies in the Parables of Jesus* (Nashville: Abingdon-Cokesbury Press, 1917), p. 80.

41. Catherine Marshall, *Something More* (Carmel, New York: Guideposts Associates, Inc. 1974), p. 42.

42. Catherine Marshall, *Adventures in Prayer* (Old Tappan, New Jersey: Fleming H. Revell Co., 1975), p. 82.

43. Thomas Merton quoted in an article by C. Gordon Peerman, *Weavings* magazine (Nashville, Tennessee: The Upper Room, Vol. VII, No. 2, 1992), pp. 38-39.

44. *Op cit*, Fred Luskin, pp. 68-69.

45. *Ibid*, p. xii.

46. *Ibid*, p. 9.

47. *Ibid*, pp. 176-177.

48. William Barclay, *The Gospel of John*, Vol. 2, The Daily Bible Study Series (Philadelphia: Westminster Press, 1956), pp. 8-9.

49. *Op cit*, Dunnam and Reisman, pp. 118-119.

50. *The Interpreter's Dictionary of the Bible*, Vol. A-D (Nashville: Abingdon Press, 1962), article by S. J. DeVries, "Blasphemy," p. 445.

51. *The Interpreter's Bible*, Vol. VIII (Nashville: Abingdon-Cokesbury Press, 1952), p. 224.

52. *A Theological Word Book of the Bible* (New York: The Macmillan Company, 1956), p. 32.

53. George A. Maloney, *Your Sins Are Forgiven You* (New York: Alba House, 1994), p. 8.

54. *Op cit*, James K. Wagner, *An Adventure in Healing and Wholeness*, p. 122.

55. *Op cit*, George A. Maloney, *Your Sins Are Forgiven You*, p. 2.

56. John Sutherland Bonnell, *Do You Want To Be Healed?* (New York: Harper & Row Publishers, 1968), p. 91.

57. William Barclay, *The Gospel of Luke*, The Daily Bible Study Series, (Philadelphia: Westminster Press, 1956), pp. 211-212.

58. *Ibid*, p. 213.

59. *Op cit, The Interpreter's Bible*, Vol. VIII, p. 279.

60. Henri Nouwen, *The Return of the Prodigal Son* (New York: Doubleday, 1992), p. 123.

61. *Ibid*, p. 123.

62. *Ibid*, p. 130.

63. Leonard J. Biallas, *World Religions* (Mystic, Connecticut: Twenty-Third Publishing, 1991), p. 117.

64. *Op cit*, Flora S. Wuellner, *Forgiveness, The Passionate Journey*, p. 19.

65. David N. Freedman and Michael J. McClymond, *The Rivers of Paradise* (Grand Rapids, Michigan: W. B. Eerdmans, 2001), p. 436.

66. *Op cit*, Flora S. Wuellner, *Forgiveness, The Passionate Journey*, pp. 19-20.

67. Corrie ten Boom, *The Hiding Place* (Washington Depot, Connecticut: Chosen Books, 1971), p. 215.

68. The *Columbus Dispatch*, Columbus, Ohio, article by Terry Mattingly, October 12, 2001.

69. *Op cit*, James K. Wagner, *Blessed To Be A Blessing*, p. 86.

70. *Op cit*, Flora S. Wuellner, *Forgiveness, the Passionate Journey*, p. 155.

71. Danny E. Morris, from his unpublished manuscript, "Anatomy of Forgiveness," written in 1999.

72. *Op cit*, James K. Wagner, *An Adventure in Healing and Wholeness*, pp. 60-61.

Printed in the United States
217050BV00004B/2/P

9 780788 024375